TALES FOR BEGINNERS

by

Greville Edgecombe

First published 2003
Revised edition published in 2014
by Ross Mallock
Goose Cottage
Thruxton
Andover
Hamphire SP11 8NF

ISBN 978-1-291-72499-8

# CONTENTS

Foreword by HRH The Prince of Wales KG KT GCB AK QSO ADC
Colonel-in-Chief, The Army Air Corps

Foreword by HRH The Prince of Wales KG KT GCB AK QSO ADC
Colonel-in-Chief, The Army Air Corps

## CLARENCE HOUSE

As Colonel-in-Chief of the Army Air Corps, I am lucky enough to see the regimental magazines which are issued to both serving and retired members of the Corps throughout the year. The Army Air Corps Newsletter appears every three months and the Corps Journal, a substantial full-colour publication, comes out annually in July.

These periodicals record the activities, adventures and issues facing Army Aviation around the world and they make fascinating reading, contributed by people right across the spectrum of rank, age and experience.

The late Lieutenant Colonel Greville Edgecombe wrote a series of Kiplingesque stories for the Newsletter between 1984 and 1989, which were so timelessly popular that they were subsequently republished shortly after his untimely death in 1997.

Greville spent the first twelve years of his boyhood in India and it is no surprise that Kipling's 'Just So Stories' enjoyed a special place in his heart. Towards the end of his Army service, when he was intimately involved in flight safety matters at Middle Wallop, he began this series of cautionary tales to emphasise the unforgiving nature of flying as a profession. Typically, though, the message is put across with great humour and humanity, much of it at the author's expense! Indeed, it is easy to overlook the fact that this catalogue of near-disasters conceals a distinguished flying career in which his determination and courage, particularly in Aden, became legendary within the Army Air Corps.

I was delighted when the editor of the Army Air Corps Newsletter and Journal agreed that it was high time that these entertaining stories should be collected in one volume, peppered with Greville's own puckish illustrations.

In my view, a copy of *Tales for Beginners* should be carried in every flying suit, to be dipped into by the wearer whenever the opportunity presents itself!

The beginner at his Wings Parade, 1960. Note that Dilly Edgecombe (the Jack Russell) is in the reluctant custody of Capt D M McAllister RA, Course Instructor, purely in the interests of symmetry

The Army aviator, deep in thought

The Flight Commander, Aden 1966, in his element

The offshore skipper, 1994

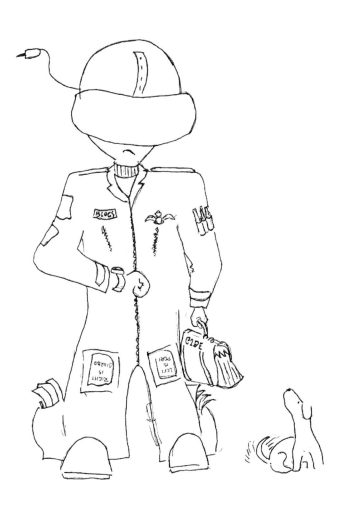

Blogs is a flier. He has wings where most people keep a hanky, a big watch, a big bag and pockets stuffed full to keep his feet on the ground. He also has a dog

## SIR IN A VERY BLACK MOOD

Many moons ago, oh my best beloved, when I was a fledgling just off the fixed wing perch, there was a very senior officer who required to be taken from Tidworth to Hawkinge (an airfield, oh my best beloved—clearings and LPs had not been thought of then).

The Squadron Guru cast around for someone to do the task but everyone knew the 'VSO' and found business elsewhere. The Guru's eyes fell upon me—in my new flying suit, a shiny infantry officer full of the latest techniques—and they lit up. The sky was clear and hardly a breath of air rustled the grass. 'Even he', mused the Guru, 'though not Passenger Qualified, let alone VIP rated (note the era), could not possibly muck up such a simple thing under these conditions'.

'Go forth and take the Great Man to Hawkinge and then bring him back again.' he ordered.

Now that may sound a simple task, as you can well understand, oh my best beloved, but the Guru had forgotten two things, and so had I.

First: the Great Man wanted to return at 6 o'clock the next morning to be back in time to review his troops.

Second: clear skies and light winds—the significance of which you, of course, oh my best beloved, are well aware of?

The trip there was perfect and speedy, and the Great Man was well pleased. He even inadvertently let slip a small compliment. The next morning hardly even dawned—it was like pea soup! I stumbled out to my aeroplane, just to show form, even knowing that the Great Man understood these things and was still safely tucked up in bed. He was not, oh my best beloved, he was stomping round the aircraft in the murk looking at his watch, looking very angry and looking very senior.

'You are late!' he snapped, 'Let's go'. Such a man knew everything and was not to be argued with, so go we did.

The next two hours were a nightmare. Occasional sightings of railway lines, a long runway appearing at right angles directly underneath (you, oh my best beloved, know well that Gatwick's runway lies in the same direction as that in which I required to go) and to cap it all my VSO opened a crisp, well-ironed copy of The Times at the leader page, and what few instruments that were provided for me disappeared from view. I fear, oh my best beloved, that I lacked the courage to comment, for Sir was fairly obviously in a very black mood. Suddenly, when all seemed lost, the VSO turned back the left hand corner of his paper (not my side), glanced out of the window and said 'Well—my car's there. At least somebody is on time'.

Little did he know that he had given me the first inkling that we had arrived at Bulford Strip.

I landed somehow in a welter of sweat, opened the door for him and stood at the salute as I had seen pictures of very smart RAF Royal Flight officers doing, but with my knees knocking, my hand shaking and my lips dry to cracking point.

After he had gone I dared not take off again to return to Wallop until the visibility had cleared to at least faintly VFR conditions. Sanity had returned.

*Pick over what bones you like out of that one, oh my best beloved. But then you would never let yourself get into a situation like that, would you?*

# WHERE'S THE GENERAL?

Many years ago, oh my best beloved, you may remember that I was tasked to take a singularly senior officer to Hawkinge and back just prior to acquiring my Passenger Qualification. The sequel to this was that my OC invited me to do some revision, to retrace my steps and sort out my navigation. It was to be a straight there-and-back sortie, the weather was cold but clear, and the sky matched my Blue Instrument Rating Card exactly.

Nothing could go wrong this time. My Battalion, which I had recently left, had moved to Shorncliffe so I rang a fellow subaltern, invited myself to lunch, settled my Jack Russell terrier comfortably on the back seat and set off.

The navigation was spot on, the landing was nigh on perfect and I taxied into dispersal somewhat smugly, under the admiring gaze of two senior-looking RAF officers in long grey greatcoats reaching almost down to the ground, and caps with the peaks glistening with gold braid. I was a little surprised, as I climbed out, to see the two stride up, halt with commendable precision and salute in impeccable unison. The landing wasn't *that* good, oh my best beloved, and I should have smelt a rat!

'Good morning, sir,' said the more senior looking, 'Welcome to Hawkinge. Can we be of any assistance? Do you require transport?'

So *this* was the flying world! As I stripped off my flying suit, revealing my immaculate Service Dress and gleaming pips and returned the salute, I was glad I had dressed appropriately and bulled my brown shoes to a mahogany glow.

'Oh' said one of them.

'Where's the General?' said the other.

'My God!' said I, 'I forgot all about him!'

Springing to the rear door of the aircraft, I opened it and cracked up my best Sovereign's Parade salute. Out hopped the terrier, inspected my two visitors laconically, and then squatted down and answered an urgent and major call of nature at their feet.

There was a long pause during which unimaginable expressions passed across the faces of the two in front of me, then they wheeled about in absolute silence and strode away. I was still gazing after them rather perplexedly when my friend slipped out from behind a bush, grinning broadly.

'I wonder what all that was about?' I said.

He had the grace to blush and said 'When I clocked in to meet you they wanted to know why you were coming, so I said you were probably bringing the General.'

This completed my PQ and I was shortly afterwards sent to Kenya, there being nowhere further away my OC could send me at short notice.

*Now the moral of this story, oh my best beloved, is do not believe the old adage about not fouling your own doorstep. The smell is far more penetrating if you foul someone else's.*

# THE SPUR OF THE MOMENT

Aeons ago, oh my best beloved, when your egg had not been laid and mine was but newly hatched, though my wings were still fixed firmly to my body, my Master grew impatient with me because of the insignificant altercations with two great men which I have mentioned previously. He decided that I needed to gain experience in some far distant land, and the further away the more relaxed and contented he would be.

Now my Master was a Major, and in those days, oh my best beloved, a Major wielded much power—roughly akin to a modern AAC Brigadier. This one, for instance, controlled a squadron of four flights, each of three Austers and three Skeeters at Middle Wallop, another similar flight in Northern Ireland, a flight in Cyprus, one in Libya and one in Kenya. Now Kenya, you will appreciate, oh my best beloved, was the farthest away of all, so there he sent me.

It chanced that I had previously spent two years in Kenya with my Battalion hunting Mau Mau—a breed of animal now extinct in Kenya but still found in abundance in Northern Ireland—and the opportunity to fly round it, rather than walk, was heavenly retribution for my paltry failings. Even better, my Battalion from which I had so recently made my tearful departure, had just been posted back there and would no doubt much appreciate my services.

As it happened my first task was to join them hunting *Shifta*, a marauding breed of Mau Mau-like animal whose habitat is in the Northern Frontier Province north of Wajir. (Incidentally, oh my best beloved, there was a yacht club at Wajir, the Royal Wajir Yacht Club no less. There were only two members, it owned no boat, the area is semi desert, and the nearest water is over 300 miles away.)

I spent three idyllic weeks playing at cat and mouse, and when the operation ended I set off back to Nairobi, my cup of gladness overflowing. My track happened to take me over the Battalion's camp at Gil Gil and, on the spur of the moment, knowing the whole Battalion was on the road behind me, that the friend who had been the cause of my previous downfall was in camp on his own, and it was lunch time, I slipped a smoke grenade out of the rack beside me and lobbed it over the side.

Be advised *now*, oh my best beloved, before it is too late. If you are ever tempted to transgress, think first and consider every angle before you act. Half a pound of grenade starting at 70 knots and accelerating at 32 ft/sec/sec is, if nothing else, a lethal missile and once it is launched it is too late for regrets. I watched the green smoking projectile curving downwards and at the same time noticed a familiar figure emerging from the Officer's Mess door looking upwards at me, glass in hand.

To my horror the two were on a collision course. After what seemed an age the figure realised the danger and bolted back inside the door but failed to close it. The grenade hit the ground and bounced in after him. The last I saw, to my immense relief, was the fast re-emerging figure, closely followed by clouds of green smoke billowing from every door and window.

The effect inside was evidently devastating but this time my friend proved to be a friend indeed. He explained to the sceptical CO on his return that he had decided to redecorate the dining room and ante room green while the Battalion were away 'Just to freshen the place up a bit'.

*The angels were truly on my side, oh my best beloved, for I might sadly have been sword and medals at his funeral!*

# A LITTLE VOICE OF SANITY

There are so many pitfalls awaiting you, oh my best beloved, and a word in time might save you from one of them. You may remember the unfortunate misunderstanding which brought about my move to far-flung corners of the Empire and, once there, the small matter of redecorating the interior of an Officers' Mess with a remarkable feat of accurate flying. It happened, at a subsequent Regimental Dinner, that both my late CO and my current Brigade Commander simultaneously became aware of the true nature of the artwork and, while secretly admiring my skill, they cast doubts on my parentage and my future in the service. It became pressing to exonerate my good name as a matter of urgency especially as confidential report time was approaching.

The opportunity came swiftly. The whole Brigade was launched on a three-week flag-waving exercise to show the natives the might of the sword. With each move the Brigadier, an enthusiast for his aviation support, gave orders straight out of Army Aviation Pamphlet No 1(1954): *The Recce Flight will find a landing strip in grid square 1234 and Brigade HQ will set up alongside'.*

My moment had come, for I was the recce pilot and I was to be launched ahead of each move to find a roost in the selected grid square. Now whether or not the Brigadier selected his square with malice aforethought I know not, but he had an unerring instinct for the game. After the Brigade's fourth unaccompanied move, and during my fifth unsuccessful recce over impenetrable scrub, I was disconsolately sitting on the wing of my Auster in the street of a small village, pouring in a debi (flimsy 5 gallon can) of AVGAS and contemplating my future in civil life, when my late CO drove up. I doused my cigarette on the side of the debi and offered him a Coke from the old crone in the 'dookah' (local excuse for a shop) alongside.

'Not found anywhere yet, lad?' he said with a nasty grin on his dust-coated face,

...disconsolately sitting on the wing of my Auster

'better pull your socks up. Old Jacko's in a black mood and your reputation, and the Flight's, are hardly glowing!' He drove off in a cloud of dust with a wave before I realised I had no money to pay for the drinks.

Shortly thereafter I found myself in desperation orbiting a *shamba* (an area of cultivation with huts round it, oh my best beloved). It was clearly too small and totally unsuitable, but it was the only clear space for miles, and desperation breeds strange bedfellows.

I found myself on finals with a little voice of sanity on my shoulder screaming 'No! No!' I closed my ears, gritted my teeth and pressed on—full flap, just off the stall—and flopped down. The next few seconds were a whirl of red dust and skittled tree stumps before I came to rest and switched off. I climbed out and surveyed the scene, a confined area that even one of your modern rotorcraft would have been proud to have got into. Thank God for the termites which had eaten the roots of the stumps so that they just bowled over as I hit them.

A few dents in the tail plane but nothing bad—but what a place! How on earth had I missed all those antbear holes but, above all, how on earth to get out again? This was the end, the end of everything, what a recovery job! Did they still drum people out? Why hadn't I listened to the voice of reason? Shades of Jinx Jenks and Tom Pierce whispering in my ear. You may appreciate, oh my best beloved, that I had made a grave tactical error.

I was soon surrounded by friendly, admiring *wahtu* (people) who couldn't believe their eyes, or the *ndege* (bird) in their midst, and I had problems stopping them dismembering it.

Over a bowl of sour camel's milk mixed with urine, my courage and determination were regenerated. Hell, I had got myself into this mess; I'd get myself out of it. Damn the Brigadier, and the rest of them!

This, oh my best beloved, is the stuff that brave men are made of. I selected the longest possible run, unavoidably ending between the two largest huts. I gathered my forces, women and children included, gave out my orders and we all set out screaming with delight to execute the plan. We removed all the remaining tree stumps along the take-off run and filled in all the antbear holes—all, that is, except one gaping crater towards the end of the run which would have taken a Sapper troop, with plant, to fill. I detailed an old man to stand on the edge of that, stand fast as I came towards him, and then jump into the hole when I waved out of the window. The whole throng dragged the Auster back across the *shamba*, chanting in 'Sanders of the River' fashion, and pulled the tail back into the bush right up to the wing roots. I detailed four likely lads to hang on to the tail until I waved 'Let go'.

The aircraft did not quite leap forward as it had at Wallop. I lumbered slowly forward, gradually gathering speed. This was partially due to the soft dusty ground, and partially due to the fact that my four doughty warriors, their eyes full of dust and slipstream, were still hanging on to the tail like grim death.

I should have stopped and tried again, if not stopped altogether, oh my best beloved, but my mind was set and I pressed grimly on. We shook them off one after another, the *ndege* and I, and rumbling on. The old man was getting uncomfortably close and I could now clearly see the whites of his eyes and the hole beside him, so I waved. He waved back! The wheels left the ground and I caught a glimpse of him falling backwards as I passed. Whether he jumped or was knocked backwards I know not for by now the huts were looming up close. There was an audible crunching noise as the starboard wheel dragged through the thatch of one of them, and we were clear. I inspected the site from above and noted my tracks with awe. The old man was still down his hole and there was not much thatch left on his roof. And then, after a quick impromptu flying display to thank my new friends, I returned to the Flight to report—well, just another failure!

*The angels were on my side, but I wonder just how many of them it took to ensure my survival. You, who are a discerning soul, oh my best beloved, could no doubt count them.*

# WHERE ARE WE NOW?

B e aware, oh my best beloved, that what may be normal and routine to you may strike terror into the heart of lesser mortals.

I once had to take a reasonably senior personage from Mombasa to Nairobi, a distance of some 270 miles over totally featureless brush land. We soon exhausted the entertainment of spotting big game and settled deeper and deeper into an uncomfortable reverie dulled by the unsilenced roar of the mighty Bombardier engine.

Eventually my passenger, easing from one numb cheek to the other, remarked conversationally 'Beats me how you chaps find your way around. Where are we now?'

Since my map, being quite unnecessary, was in my pocket, I turned to him and foolishly said in a calculatedly anxious voice, 'Don't ask me. You're doing the map reading, aren't you?'

There was a long silence. The whole atmosphere in the cab suddenly changed. My passenger paled visibly, stammered for a while, and then croaked, 'No I haven't been doing the map reading! I haven't even got a map!'

'What!' I cried, rising to the occasion, 'My God! Where are we? I don't recognise a thing!'

At this my passenger began to gibber faintly and then his eyes lit upon a map on the pocket of his door. With shaking hands he pulled it out and thrust it towards me, a sweaty, desperate, hopeful expression on his face. I scanned the part nearest to me, and then with a frantic cry of 'We're not on this bit!' I tore it off and threw it out of the window.

'Nor this. Nor this,' and I did the same again and again.

I was finally left with a piece of map about the size of a postage stamp in my hand, and with a last despairing cry of 'We're not on any of it. We're lost!' that too went out of the window. My passenger turned an awful shade of green, his eyes rolling in his head, he shrivelled back into his seat like a little old man and then, to my horror, he was sick!

The remainder of the trip was difficult. I tried to restore his confidence and manhood by pointing out the Mombasa to Nairobi railway line and chatting brightly about this and that, but he was a broken man. Even the sight of the Ngong hills on the horizon failed to cheer him.

He left without a word when we landed. We never met again. I wonder what became of him. Consider the possibilities: I could have ruined his whole life. On the other hand, he could have become a General and ruined mine.

*Stranger things have happened, oh my best beloved, so have a care.*

# THERE! BEAT THAT!

There was a time, oh my best beloved, when aeroplanes did not cost the king's ransom they do today; these days a king would be unlikely to fetch such a price. Added to that, the aviator was looked on by the uninitiated as something of an oddball and was expected to display a degree of élan and eccentricity. For example, one Army aviator in Sycamore days, tasked to pick up the Chief of the General Staff from in front of the grandstand at the conclusion of a major military demonstration, suffered ground resonance on landing. His Sycamore shook itself to death, finally disintegrating into a heap of spare parts in front of the admiring audience. Nothing abashed, he extracted himself from the remains, marched briskly up to the grandstand, halted, transferred the cyclic stick and its attached wiring from his right to his left, saluted smartly and announced loudly, 'Your helicopter, sir—but perhaps I had better go and get you another one.' You may, oh my best beloved, be interested in the great man's reply which was 'Thank you, Mike, but I think I'll go by car.' He did, and lived to enjoy his retirement.

These factors did breed a certain cavalier charisma that at times resulted in some interesting, impromptu flying demonstrations and feats which would curl the toes of today's flight safety industry. It came to my ears that my revered master of previous tales, whose unwarranted displeasure had led to my happy banishment to Kenya, was himself not entirely blameless in this respect. It transpired that when he ran a flight in Tripoli he instigated, among other things, a short landing competition to sharpen up his little band.

In those days, fixed wing pilots were trained to touch down in a 'box' some ten yards long, marked out at the start of a short landing strip, and thereafter to stop in the shortest possible distance. The observant among you, as no doubt you are, oh my best beloved, will have noticed the remains of these strips around the perimeter track at Wallop. Not content with this well-tried system, he rigged up two tall poles with a string stretched between their tops on his selected piece of desert. The winner would be the one to touch down nearest the reverse side of the string, with bonus points for the shortest landing run.

The day dawned, the competition was keen, and he watched each gladiator in turn stagger in over the string and flop down closer and closer to it until, with some remarkable results to beat, it was finally his own turn. Not to be outdone by his juniors, he set himself up on what today would be called a 'steep sight picture approach.'

As he came over the string his aircraft staggered, stalled and fell out of the sky like a brick. It came to rest after a vertical dead stop, in a cloud of dust, flat on its belly with its wings draped like washing over the ground and only two bumps in the upper surface to show where the wheels were. My leader climbed out of the wreckage, hurried anxiously to the back and, unabashed, carefully assessed the angle of the line from the extremity of the tail up to the string above. It was absolutely vertical. Letting out a whoop of delight, he turned in triumph to the admiring throng and said, 'There—beat that, you b.......s!'

*In this short tale, oh my best beloved, I have tried to show that in endeavouring to go one better than the other fellow you could well go one worse, or that 'pride came before the fall'.*

*But on the other hand, if the worst does come to the worst, put a brave face on it—élan!*

# A SINGULARLY BEAUTIFUL PERSON

You may remember, oh my best beloved, my inadvertent destruction of a passenger's manhood during a trip from Zanzibar to Nairobi. You should be aware that the average passenger casts himself completely into your hands from the moment he reports in but, at the same time, he forms a sort of one man inspection team whose arbitrary judgement is noised abroad rather more liberally than any official report. How you and your unit treat him throughout his stay could make or mar you and your unit's reputation. There is more than one way to kill a cat as you shall hear, oh my best beloved.

The Flight was supporting a Shifta (Somali raiders) hunting expedition in the Northern Frontier Province when the GOC came to see how things were going. The RAF delivered him and his party to our strip and we ferried them around the various forward locations by Beaver. Unfortunately his ADC appeared to be surplus to requirement and, as he climbed aboard, the GOC turned to me and said, 'Look after my ADC will you. Show him as much as you can.'

Now the GOC had recently acquired a new ADC, a singularly beautiful person immaculately turned out in the best tradition of the Household Brigade. I had met him playing in a game of Rugby for the Kenya Harlequins against the Railway Club.

It had surprised me that he should indulge in such a brutal sport. He was our full back, and towards the very end of the match, with the score just in our favour, a huge railwayman with legs like oak trees and arms like pistons, broke through and thundered down on him.

Anthony (I believe that was his name), judging his moment to perfection, flung himself to one side in the nick of time. The inevitable try between the posts was converted and we lost. As we walked dejectedly off the pitch he, quite unabashed by his role in our defeat, said chattily to our captain, a white hunter of incredible valour, 'I say—do you play Polo?'

He was that sort of person, oh my best beloved.

Anthony looked magnificent in flat hat, glowing mahogany shoes and a well starched bush jacket with knife edge creases and groups of huge, gleaming buttons down the front. He was a credit to his manservant. The first and obvious thing to do with him was to give him a flight, so I strapped him into the front seat of an Auster, doors off as normal, and waved him goodbye.

Now the Auster IX, or rather the Bombardier engine, had a nasty habit called 'oil gulping'. Why 'gulping' and not 'vomiting' defeats me for, much like a seasick sailor, without any warning it would suddenly spew the entire contents of its stomach over the side—the passenger side. As it taxied in on return I looked with horror at the oil-smothered side of the aircraft, and as he emerged my worst fears were realised. Anthony looked like a badly bedraggled minstrel. He was a total ruin. Even his beautiful blond locks were a swept-back, rigid, black cockade, and the clouds of red murram dust and debris kicked up in taxiing had stuck to him and finished off the picture of a well executed tar and feathering.

What to do? I was still dithering when the REME came to my rescue in the form of the incomparable Cpl Roberts. He stepped past me, halted with a crash in front of Anthony, and swept up an incredible salute which left me speechless with amazement and admiration.

'Got ourselves into a wee bit of a mess, haven't we, sir?' he said sweetly. 'Give me your jacket and trousers and we'll have you straightened out for the General in just a jiffy.'

With that he had Anthony, uncomplaining, out of his hat and uniform and into a pair of his own PT shorts in a twinkling. He disappeared bearing the ullage in the direction of the REME tent. The Admirable Crichton could not have done better, oh my best beloved.

Anthony's skin had clearly never been exposed before and his naked torso and legs gleamed white in the equatorial sunshine as we wandered around doing this and that for the rest of the afternoon, waiting for the return of his uniform and his master.

We found a giant tortoise and Anthony picked it up for closer examination. Now tortoises are used to being horizontal, oh my best beloved, and on being rudely up-ended the strain was too much for this one. It too emptied the entire contents of its capacious bowels down the luckless Anthony's front. A more foul-smelling goo I have never come across before or since. It was as I was dabbing at him hopelessly with my handkerchief that he first screamed, and I realised that he was no longer white but a livid, lobster red.

Just at that moment we heard the drone of the approaching Beaver's engine, and with that the Admirable Crichton reappeared at the double with the uniform.

Uniform! There was only one thing uniform about it. The REME had clearly used a bucket of Avgas and swilled the whole outfit around in it, reducing it to a homogeneous green-grey, crumpled, soggy, fuming mess. However, it was too late for recriminations, the Beaver was landing and the ADC was required to jump in.

Cpl Roberts eased Anthony deftly back into his kit—and that was the second time he screamed. Avgas and sunburn are not good bedfllows.

With a whispered, 'You won't smoke, will you, sir?' Roberts tactfully disappeared and left me alone to return the General his property. The expression on the GOC's face when he saw Anthony was incredulous, but it changed to horror as I pushed the reeking, writhing body in alongside him and shut the door. Once again I found myself contemplating an early return to civil life.

All's well that ends well. I met the General again shortly afterwards and, much to my surprise, with a twinkle in his eye he said, 'Well you certainly sorted him out, didn't you? How on earth did you arrange it?'

From then until my departure the Flight could do no wrong.

*The Lord disposes in wondrous ways, oh my best beloved, but do take good care of your passengers—you may not be quite so lucky.*

# A POLICEMAN'S LOT

My banishment to Kenya, oh my best beloved, did not include my wife, so being footloose and fancy free I was something of a boon to the permanent residents of 8 Flight as I volunteered for anything and everything.

This allowed the Flight motor racing teams of Captains Barry-Taylor (Alvis) and Wright (Wright MG Special), with their respective REME pit teams, to concentrate on the serious business of competing on the various Kenya motor sports circuits.

It was thus, oh my best beloved, that I found myself on yet another *Shifta* (Bandit) hunting expedition in the Northern Frontier District (NFD). My detachment consisted of me with Auster IX XN440, a technician and a driver with a 3 ton truck containing fuel, water, food and a tent. We were attached to a company of 11 Battalion King's African Rifles and were joined by a Kenya Regiment Major, together with the local British policeman and a detachment of police askaris. We based ourselves on the village of Boona which was astride the Murram road across the semi-arid plains.

On landing, I met up with the Kenya Regiment Officer, Ray Nightingale, a game warden by trade. He had just arrived in a Landrover, in the back of which was a somewhat rickety homemade wooden cage containing a large, angry, spitting leopard. Not wishing to appear naïve, I asked casually, as Englishmen tend to do, where he had got it. He replied, equally casually, that he had caught it on the way up. Seeing it disappear into a bush not far from the road, he had stopped the Landrover, determined to catch it as a replacement for the 5 KAR leopard mascot which had recently died. Armed with a stout forked stick and accompanied by his driver and batman, he had surrounded the bush and crawled in. He jammed the stick over the leopard's head; at the same time the driver grabbed the other extremity and pulled, while the batman trussed it up. As simple as that! Incidentally he invited me to fly it back to Nairobi at the end of the exercise and, loath to seem wet, I agreed. Fortunately when it came to the crunch they could not get the leopard in.

The policeman was wildly enthusiastic about flying but he had never been in an aeroplane in his life. He had been saving all his money for some time (not that there was anything to spend it on in the NFD) to go to Nairobi to take flying lessons. My arrival was an opportunity for his first flight. Now the reason why we had selected Boona as a base, oh my best beloved, was that it was the only place in the area where the road was wide enough for the wings of the Auster to clear the surrounding bush. The slight snag was that the makeshift airstrip continued on through the village. This included a bend in the road which necessitated an equivalent bend in the take-off path. Prior to departure a police askari was dispatched to warn the *Watu* (people) in the village of our impending departure. We trundled onto the road, stood on the brakes, wound up the Bombardier engine, and let go.

On reflection, I suppose that an aeroplane taking off through the middle of a remote Turkana village was about as unusual as the same thing happening in Oxford Street, but this didn't occur to me at the time. It was certainly too much for the locals, who rushed out into the road to watch and cheer.

We met the locals when I was about two feet clear of the ground and about to negotiate the bend. Now you will appreciate, oh my best beloved, that my concentration at that time was a little taken up with things other than my passenger. I was therefore somewhat surprised as I banked into the bend, desperately trying not to scythe down the mob with my wing tip, to find his head and shoulders

My MIND WAS A LITTLE TAKEN UP
WITH THINGS OTHER THAN MY PASSENGER

GJDC

arrive in my lap.

'Not now!' I snarled, but then as the aircraft straightened up, so did he. Another bank and over he went again. It was just like one of those stand-up toys! He had the most incredible vertigo I have ever come across, or was it a spatial disorientation? We tried all sorts of things to break him of it (at his request of course) including flying low level, steeply banked, over the edge of a 1000-foot cliff, a loop or two and even flying through a cloud, but to no avail. He went ashen grey and absolutely rigid, saying he felt as if he was falling down a bottomless black hole. The most he could take was about 20 feet above obstacle level and very flat, unbanked, skidding turns.

Thus we continued for the rest of the day. Later we landed by the Dobell Wells. Myth has it, oh my best beloved, that these were dug in ancient times by a race of giants. They go down some hundreds of feet through solid rock. The shafts are neither uniform nor vertical but snake crazily downwards. Crooked poles, or rather branches, were positioned across the shaft about every ten feet, set loosely in niches cut into the walls. Getting from one to another was via more inverted, forked branches. These hung by their forks, swinging free, hooked over each cross member, with their long ends dangling down to the one below.

Water was drawn by girls of the tribe, who, positioned on each horizontal pole, passed the water up in small buckets from hand to hand. At the top, the water was tipped into a channel which fed a trough at the bottom of a huge wedge-shaped cutting dug into the ground. Camels were herded down into the cutting where, one at a time, they could reach the trough, drink their fill and climb up the other side. Since a thirsty camel can slurp a dozen or more full buckets without noticing them, you will appreciate, oh my best beloved, that watering a herd of a hundred or more camels can be a laborious process, even without 'bricking' them.

I decided to explore one of the wells to see what it was like. It was chilly, damp and dark. Over the ages the rock sides had been polished smooth by countless naked bodies. Tiny sounds echoed eerily up out of the darkness below. A slip meant a long untidy fall. Much to my surprise, the policeman came too. He set off with alacrity sliding down the rickety wet dangling branches, continuing from one to the other into the black abyss without a tremor. So much for his vertigo!

He never went for flying lessons, oh my best beloved. After a couple of further trips he realised his limitations and turned to pot holing. We did, however, have a remarkable binge on his savings at the Royal Wajir Yacht Club.

The *Watu* in the village? Well, luckily they all enjoyed the show and survived.

*No doubt you, oh my best beloved, always clear your take off and landing path as carefully as I did thereafter.*

# AN URGENT CRY

We all have our own idiosyncrasies, some more than others, but none more than the three Services. I believe, oh my best beloved, that it is time that you learned something about these, for many are the pitfalls for those who tread paths unfamiliar to them.

It is a brave or foolhardy man who dabbles in another Service's magic—especially on their own ground. For instance, the Royal Navy has its own unique way of bringing ships into harbour. I was introduced to the method as a cadet at Sandhurst on a familiarisation visit to a ship at Portsmouth in what must have been the dead of winter. The system simply involved lining every available hand along the rail, in their shirtsleeves, in wind, spray and sleet from Spithead until safely tied up alongside an hour or so later. It seemed to work admirably for them. I subsequently tried it on a Joint Services yacht at Hornet with singularly little success. Being completely unsighted by the mass of bodies, I motored into a pontoon at some speed. The crew all fell over the side under the nose of the Captain In Charge.

On my Fixed Wing Pilots Course my RAF instructor taught me a strange RAF 'ju-ju' which he guaranteed would give a 'first time' engine start every time. It involved thrusting your arm out of the window and, at the psychological moment, with thumb pointing towards the ground, chanting:

*'Switchesoffuelonthrottleclosedbrakeshardon!'*

This urgent cry was taken up and repeated by a man outside, then you caught both the aeroplane and the observer by surprise by reversing your thumb, screaming 'Contact', and pressing the starter button. The effect was miraculous. I followed the drill religiously with great success thereafter—that is, until my first away visit in an Auster to an RAF airfield.

I had to deliver a cavalry officer to RAF Valley. The trip there was somewhat draining—but more of that another time—so I stayed the night.

Next morning when I went to start up, I had a real live RAF 'Erk' in attendance. My moment had come. Anxious to impress, I did a silent rehearsal; then went into my RAF starting ritual.

*'Switchesoffuelonthrottleclosedbrakeshardon!'* I intoned, arm thrust out rigidly and thumb smartly at right angles to it.

'Eh?' said the 'Erk', looking puzzled.

I whipped back my hand and desperately checked my lines for an embarrassing mistake. No, they were just as Flt Lt 'Crabair' had taught me. Perhaps I had mumbled them. I tried again:

'Switches off...Fuel on...Throttle closed...Brakes hard on!'

I enunciated as clearly as possible, looking him straight in the face.

'Erk' looked at me for a long moment, his brain visibly churning over. Then he walked over, stuck his head in through my window and said scornfully:

'Listen 'ere, mate! I got this fing thing out of its cornflakes packet for yer. Got ye into it. What the 'eck do ye want me ter do now—*'and launch yer?'*

# OTHER MEN'S MEDICINE

You may remember, oh my best beloved, that I warned you against the dangers of imitating customs of the other Services; you now know that RAF starting procedures and the Naval system of bringing a ship into harbour can sometimes lead you into embarrassing and mortifying situations.

Not all that long ago (but probably while you were still at your mother's knee), I was involved in that confusing drama (half-way between peace-keeping and withdrawal), the Aden campaign. I commanded a flight of six Scouts. There were two flights operating in the theatre: 8 Flight (which was mine) and 13 Flight. Flights used to divide their time between being 'up country' in 'Area West' (the main operational area) and the base at Little Aden. The 'down country' flight was responsible for providing several single-aircraft detachments around the Protectorate for operations in Aden itself, and for the usual 'cabbying' or liaison sorties for the gilded staff.

The Flights used to spend about eight to ten weeks 'up country' turn and turn about. The trick was to extend your spell up there, away from Wing Headquarters, for as long as possible. At this I was singularly successful. It is quite remarkable how you can stretch out a vital operation if you try hard enough. It's a trick well worth learning, oh my best beloved. Filibustering, I believe it's called.

During one of my enforced spells at base under the direct supervision of the CO, the Sultan of Oman discovered that the 'Aden disease' (irregular invasion) had taken over in Socotra, a large island off the horn of Africa, which he owned. It was decided to send a gunboat and a company of the Welsh Guards to root out the rebels and liberate the people.

Since none of the current stock of RN gunboats had a suitable or serviceable helicopter on board at the time, it was decided that I should 'take ship' and act as 'point' in the assault. I was sent to liaise with the Captain of the selected frigate to find out the form.

I was hot, dusty, crumpled and not a little soggy after the ride out through 'the chop' to the anchored ship in a grubby little *walla walla* boat. Certainly I was not in a proper state to present myself to the captain of one of Her Majesty's warships when we finally came alongside. Nothing daunted, I caught hold of the ladder and began to climb. As my head topped the gunwale, I was confronted by the shrill of bosun's pipes and the sight of a bevy of naval officers, petty officers and ratings immaculately turned out in crisp, starched, gleaming white rig; all smartly at the salute in their quaint fashion.

'My God', I thought, 'I've arrived in the middle of a parade. They must have the Admiral on board!' I was about to hurry back down the ladder to the safety of my bumboat when a little lad, with an enormous, brass-mounted telescope tucked under his arm, stepped forward.

'Aha! A Midshipman', I thought—remembering my *Hornblower*. 'Take me to your leader', I said, putting a bold face on it.

'I *am* the leader!' he replied indignantly—and indeed he was! I had forgotten that I was a field officer and all this ceremony was my rightful due. Be warned, oh my best beloved, always to polish your boots and look to the cut of your rig before ever you set foot aboard a naval vessel.

Ah! And never judge an old salt by the wrinkles on his face.

Some time later, with all that behind me, I had reason to revise my ideas. The Flight had just arrived back at Falaise from an 'up country' spell. I was dashing about getting used to the new scene, when I got instructions to take the Commander Land Forces out to lunch on board *HMS Hermes* that day.

HMS Hermes

31

I knew there was no aircraft carrier in the harbour, so, as I was about to take off on another sortie, I briefed a newly-joined subaltern to find out her location, the frequency on which she was working and her callsign, so that I could pick them up on my way to collect the General.

Now the subaltern was still a little wet behind the ears. In addition he had a slight stammer. He was, of course, a cavalryman. To be sure he got it right, I gave him a piece of paper inscribed:

HMS HERMES

LOCATION? _____

FREQUENCY? _____

CALLSIGN? _____

That seemed fairly foolproof to me. On completing my first trip I dashed back to Falaise with all too little time to get to Aden to pick up the General. As I landed, the languid figure of Ponsonby-Jones shambled out to the aircraft to meet me, clutching my piece of paper in his hand. I leaned out of the door, pulling my helmet away from my ear so that I could hear him.

'Her-Herr-Hermes i-i-isn't i-i-in the har-har-harbour,' he began, but I hadn't time for the rest. I snatched the piece of paper out of his hand. Waving him away, protesting, I raced to Aden, pulling out all the stops on the way.

Command Hill Pad was located on a precipitous, rocky hillside, at the bottom of a long flight of steps some 100 feet below the General's house. As I landed I saw his figure, immaculate in Tropical Service Dress and Sam Browne, start out down the steps towards me. I fished in my pocket and pulled out my piece of paper to brief myself. To my horror it was as blank as when I first gave it to Ponsonby-Jones. By now the General was reaching the bottom of the steps, so, putting a brave face on it, I climbed out, smiled and went round to greet him and strap him in.

As we took off I noticed the General waving at me and pointing at his ears. I had, in fact, unplugged him so that I could go into secret consultation with RAF Khormaksar regarding the location of our destination:

'For God's sake! Where's *Hermes?*'

'Well, she's on her way round from Bahrain. We don't know where she is but she must be somewhere to the East.'

'Do you know her frequency or callsign?'

'Afraid not.'

Making the best of things, I nodded to the General, secretly switching his

intercom back on, and said, 'Ah! It's working again! She's away to the East, sir. We'll soon be there.'

The air was laden with dust and visibility was minimal; the only way to find Hermes was to fly eastward just out of sight of land, thus covering as wide a swathe of navigable water as possible. We were in instrument conditions and had no life jackets on, but what's the use of a life jacket if the water is shark infested? A long time passed and the General began to fidget in his seat. Just as panic was beginning to set in—sweet music! Khormaksar came up on the air again. I hastily put the fault back into the General's intercom.

'We're not sure, but we think *Hermes* has somehow got to the *West* of us. You'd better turn round and try there if you don't want to end up in India!'

I executed a very flat, gentle about-turn (which my passenger didn't notice) and set off back the way I had come. An age passed. The General had begun to inspect his watch pointedly when—blessed relief—an aircraft carrier emerged in the limited circle of water I could see below me. With a smile to my passenger, and a sigh of relief, I began to let down towards it—but then, to my horror, a second one appeared through the murk a little further on!

What were the gods doing to me? Ship recognition had never been my forte. Which one was *Hermes*? Abandoning all pretence, I hovered round each of them in turn below deck level and told the General to look for the name written on the bow, or the bridge, or the lifeboats…anywhere!

Nothing...and then a flash of inspiration. *Hermes* was reputedly very small, and one of those carriers was smaller than the other! I poled back to the smaller one, but then (vexed question) how to communicate? Never, oh my best beloved, *never* go aboard a Royal Naval vessel (or any other vessel for that matter) without first asking permission to come aboard—but *how?*

Necessity is the mother of invention, so I drove up alongside the bridge. There, inside, was a stately figure, with gold braid up to his elbows driving his little machine, just like me.

Attracting his attention, I pointed at my passenger and then at my mouth. Quick on the uptake, he nodded, so I pointed at my aeroplane and then over his shoulder down at his deck. Once again his nimble brain got my message (he hadn't got all the braid for nothing!). He nodded, smiled and waved (thumbs up) at me.

Thankfully I flew round the island to the flight deck and landed smartly on a large circle painted on the deck with an 'H' in the middle of it. Thank heavens something was standard between the two Services! There we closed down and we waited.

You remember my arrival on the Frigate, oh my best beloved, and the

reception party that awaited me, a mere Field Officer? Well now I was waiting to give them time to assemble the twenty-one gun salute, which, no doubt, was the General's due.

A long time passed. Eventually a door on the side of the island opened and the reception partly emerged. Not the gleaming white uniforms, not the telescope; not the shrill of bosun's pipes this time, but just a little fat, bearded man in bare buff, sandals and PT shorts with his stomach hanging over his belt. I pushed my General towards him, started up, and fled in utter confusion and abject misery. I never did discover whether the General was expected to lunch or, indeed, whether he got any at all.

When I arrived home I made a light-hearted signal to the Royal Navy which read as follows:

---

**ALL YOU CHINESE LOOK THE SAME TO ME EXCLAM WHOEVER YOU WERE CMM HOPE YOU GAVE THE GENERAL A GOOD LUNCH AND SALVED MY GOOD NAME PD**

---

My signal was evidently handed to the Commander in Chief, Admiral Sir Michael Le Fanu, where it probably went down like the proverbial lead balloon on more than one account.

*You have been warned, oh my best beloved.*

*Never dabble in other men's medicine. But then you would never get yourself into a situation like that in the first place, would you?*

*Incidentally, you might pick a few more bones out of that one if you are astute.*

# THE POWER OF PRAYER

You may, oh my best beloved, remember that in a tale some time ago I mentioned a trip, taking a cavalryman from Wallop to RAF Valley, which was a trifle trying. Now that the summer months are with us perhaps you should be warned before clear skies and sunshine breed complacency in you.

One calm, sunny, summer day, I was tasked to take a cavalry Major up to RAF Valley in an Auster VI the following morning. The start was to be early, as I had to get him back the same day. Loud warning bells should have been ringing everywhere after my experience on a previous trip which I have told you about, but unlike you, oh my best beloved, some people never learn.

The next morning I could barely find my way to the airfield through the fog. When I finally found the hangar there was nobody else about, other than my passenger who, resplendent in cherry coloured trousers, Sam Browne and with dew dripping off his hat peak and eyebrows, was standing dejectedly outside the door in the soggy mist.

'I don't suppose Teeny Weeny Airways will be going anywhere today?' he said with a slight but irritating lift to one corner of his lip.

'Why not?' I replied sweetly—and instantly regretted it. 'Help me push her out and we'll be on our way.' In those days, 651 Squadron was housed in Hangar 3, one of five set out roughly in the form of an E at Middle Wallop. We pushed XP 631 onto the mist-shrouded apron between two hangars, climbed in, started up and taxied out. All went well for the first 20 yards or so, while I had the hangars dimly in view on either side of me, but as soon as we got clear of them my troubles began—and stayed with me for the rest of the day.

Away from the hangars there was nothing to see but a 50-yard radius of unrevealing grass. My plan was to taxi out to a take-off point a safe distance across the airfield, turn about to face the rising sun showing through the mist and to use that to keep me straight on my take-off path. Holding direction taxiing across the airfield was simple — the large 'P' type compass suspended from the roof, set at

270°, clearly pointed the way. But judging distance run over the ground without any reference points in sight was a different matter, and that was my problem!

I trundled slowly on and on. The back of my neck began to prickle and a slight, stinging sweat broke out on my brow as I tried anxiously to judge how far I had gone. Surely I must be about to run through the hedge on the far side of the airfield? How would I explain an upended wreck in the middle of the Wallop village school playground—no doubt the children would be delighted when they arrived! Just a few more yards very slowly, to be on the safe side, and then I would turn round—and then—just a foot or two more 'for the wife and kids'. Finally I made my decision, stopped and turned round to face the sun. There it was showing through the mist straight in front of me, a round white aiming mark to guide my path. I stood on the brakes, wound up the engine to full bore, squared my shoulders and, making my final foolish decision, I set my face firmly to the sun and let go.

Pointing at the sun, and heading 090°, we rolled gently forward gaining momentum, the prop tearing the mist back in shreds past the windscreen. We had hardly gone more than a hundred yards when we were bounced airborne by the wheels hitting the draining depression on the outer edge of the tarmac dispersal area in front of the hangars and then, almost immediately, I saw the doors of Hangars 3 and 4 flash by on either side of me.

My mind may not have been all that clear before but now it was crystal clear and working overtime: the boiler room chimney straight ahead! Ease her to the right... not too far, Hangar 5 is behind Hangar 4. I saw no more till we broke through into a clear, calm dawn above an endless sea of rolling white cloud lit to beautiful shades by the slanting sunlight. With a sigh of relief I set course for Anglesey, somewhere out there at the limit of my fuel endurance.

All went well for the next hour or so. My passenger was filled with admiration for my undoubted skill, and was profuse with his compliments before dozing comfortably off.

The navigation was going well apart from a slight, unjustified, feeling of unease somewhere at the back of my mind—after all I had carefully worked out my course the day before, and there was nothing to be seen of the ground to gainsay that. About the time when we should have been crossing into Wales, and to my delight I had my passenger fumbling sleepily for his passport, cloud began to build up in front of and above us. The day before, the met man had said that there would be 'extensive ground mist which would soon burn off'. He had been wrong about the latter so this was hardly surprising.

Now you are probably aware, oh my best beloved, that the Auster VI was not quite as well endowed for instrument flying as your modern machine. An altimeter, a compass hung upside down from the roof and viewed through a mirror, an artificial horizon that looked like a glass-entombed scarecrow, and a turn and slip indicator were all the instruments it boasted. However I was, by now, an experienced aviator with some 300 hours under my belt, five of them on instruments. I had not heard a peep out of the radio all morning, and there was nowhere else to go but onwards to where they were expecting me, so on we went. Inevitably, the cloud above and the cloud below eventually met up.

This, my first experience of entering cloud in anger, proved a little nerve-racking. The previously smooth motion changed suddenly to something akin to driving a motorbike over a ploughed field at speed, the even engine note rose periodically to a high pitched scream and my every instinct told me that I was in a tight, spiralling, diving turn and, for all I knew, I probably was.

After several occasions when I noticed my passenger apparently hanging from his straps with dust, nuts and bolts and pencil stubs passing upwards past his face, I soon got the hang of it and settled down. Foolishly I then got out my map, with its bold, black track line drawn across the middle, to reassure him. As I did so, my eye automatically caught and followed the line to where I noticed printed underneath it the words MT SNOWDON. Reassurance was not mine! I glanced hurriedly at my altimeter...2,000 feet...and then began, surreptitiously, to scratch at the pencil line to see whether there was a height printed underneath it. A few quick time and distance calculations established that we were perilously close to the mountain, so I entered a somewhat shaky full power climb.

At about the time when I estimated that we must, hopefully, be overhead Snowdon—I never did discover how high it was—the first bolt of lightning flashed past the window and hail stones streaked past n their horizontal way. By now my passenger was wide awake. I had to turn the cockpit lighting on to see him in the gloom and found that he had acquired a somewhat greenish tinge, varnished over with a shiny layer of cold sweat; and his voice had become a trifle reedy. This was hardly surprising as the scarecrow in the artificial horizon had begun desperately trying to frighten the ball and pointer out of the far side of the turn and slip indicator next door, and the altimeter needle become a blur in whichever direction it was turning.

There comes a time in most Christian men's lives when prayer becomes a pressing necessity, oh my best beloved. It came to be most recently when caught in a typhoon, in a 32-foot boat, in mid-South China Sea, and it came to me then. Not everyone is fortunate enough to have 'Him' on their side at the *moment critique*. St Paul's conversion, or the revelation to Moses on the mountain, could hardly have been more dramatic than the answer to my prayer.

Just when the bottom seemed to be about to fall out of my little world, we

burst out of the side of a towering, black, billowing, crashing precipice of cloud, into blazing sunshine and gin clear, smooth air with the Isle of Anglesey laid out like a map way below us.

We joined Valley, with the small problem of being 'No 1' in the circuit in front of four Hunters, and landed—noting with some satisfaction that they all had to peel off and go round again.

I draw a veil of silence as to how much fuel they put in to fill her up. Suffice to say that the black cliff stayed to the southeast all day and, as my passenger had already found a pressing reason to return by train, I stayed the night.

*In this day and age, you, oh my best beloved, are far too wise and well informed to get yourself into a situation like that—but, should you ever inadvertently do so, if all else fails, never forget the power of prayer!*

*If nothing else, it clears the head wonderfully.*

# THE ART OF COARSE COURSEMANSHIP

Perhaps, since these tales are intended for beginners, I had better go right back to the beginning. You will, no doubt, be encouraging others to follow your example and go flying, oh my best beloved. Be aware that there is a right way and a wrong way of doing everything and there are those who get it wrong every time, so be a little selective about whom you encourage. You may be galvanising someone into disaster.

Take, for instance, Pennington-Upton, a young man of impeccable breeding with a penchant for fast cars and their associated accoutrements. He left the Umteenth Hussars, with the Colonel's thankful blessing, and drove away to Middle Wallop to join his course. Winding down the Hampshire lanes, the wind over the drop-head blowing his and his partner's hair into his face, and with the exhilarating roar of engine and radio numbing his brain, he inadvertently drove straight over a small crossroads, failing to notice the halt sign nestling amongst the bushes. Another man might have got away with it, oh my best beloved but, unfortunately for young Upton, a small black Mini happened to be crossing on the major road at the same time.

They met with a splendid crash which booted the Mini over the hedge like a rugby ball kicked by one of your better Australian internationals. It landed on the far side with a crunch, pitch poled a few times scattering parts in all directions, and came to rest upside down in the middle of a ploughed field, like a well shot pheasant. There was a long moment of deathly stillness, punctuated by the ping of cooling metal and the gentle hiss of escaping steam.

Young Upton sat in his somewhat battered roadster at the middle of the crossroads surveying with some horror what he had done. To his immense relief, the crumpled black hulk suddenly began to rock and to emit unintelligible but decidedly profane noises. At length a door fell off and a tall, slim figure in light blue uniform and a shorter, more rotund, figure in khaki crawled out. The

former was a Squadron leader, and the latter wore a pale blue beret and the crowns and pips of a Lieutenant Colonel on the muddy wreck that had once been an immaculate and costly Service Dress. They were, in fact, the Chief Flying Instructor and his deputy fresh from appeasing a local farmer who had been outraged by the antics of a student pilot practising his new-found skill.

Surely this was a most inauspicious start to any flying career, let alone a military one.

There is one man who is a legend in the art of coursemanship: a foreign student—Yussif Bin Zulliman by name. Yussif started his military career as *chokera* (small boy) Assistant to the *cha wallah* of C Company 1st Bn The Royal Blankshire Regiment, stationed in a desert kingdom during the British mandate there. On independence—having by then risen to Chief Cha Wallah to Battalion HQ and thereby acquiring a formidable pedigree of military experience—he found himself well qualified for military stardom, and he became a Captain in the Imperial Guard.

Wallop first saw him when he arrived on a flying course with a mandate from the War Office that *he must pass,* a fortunate situation for any student. Zulliman suddenly found himself in a land of milk and honey, where beautiful, unveiled and uninhibited maidens abounded, where the nectar the natives drank sent shivers down his spine and turned his knees to jelly and where people and places had unpronounceable names like Acroyd-Hunt, Middle Wallop and Beaconsfield. Yussif Bin Zulliman had arrived at his Mecca.

A suitable instructor had to be found from the gallant band of civilian, ex-wartime, RAF fighter pilots who did the basic fixed wing instruction for the Army. With typical British flair, one Joe Ruprecht, a Polish wartime ace of incredible bravery, was selected. He had a puckish sense of humour but a somewhat limited and staccato command of the English language.

On his second day, a bewildered Zulliman, trussed up like a chicken in a harness with a bulky parachute hanging behind his knees, was led out of the hangar. Doing the Battle of Britain waddle, he was taken out to a Chipmunk, inserted with a shoehorn and strapped securely in. There he found himself alone (you, oh my best beloved, are aware that his instructor was sitting out of sight behind him) in a wonderful, silver flying machine. In front of him, myriad knobs and dials spun and danced crazily. Then, to his amazement, a distant voice, unseen, spoke in his ear in a strange tongue, 'You OK? Vee vill now staart ze machine ant go.'

Suddenly there was the repeated sound of gunfire from close by and smoke billowed past his head—you may have forgotten that the Chipmunk engine was started by a black powder 12 bore cartridge and seldom started first time. Ducking and weaving figures, holding their thumbs in the air, rushed in as if to the attack. Yussif was afraid—he would have dived for cover but he could not move because the infidel assassins had tied him to his seat—but Allah preserved him by throwing a transparent, bulletproof mantle over his head. There was a rumble and the machine rolled forward out of reach of the enemy. It snaked and bumped across the grass and then, with a terrifying roar, the ground fell away from under it altogether. A stunned Yussif Bin Zulliman was either in paradise or airborne.

Once at a good height in the clear blue sky, Joe said, 'Straight ant lewel flight...see now, ze hoorizon is paaraallil to ze vings ant cuts across ze mittle off ze bonnet? Zat is straight ant lewel attitude. Kip it so! You hef control.'

The plane wheeled and dived before Joe grabbed control again and repeated his instructions, ending with, 'Vot is ze metter?'

After a long pause, a plaintive voice came back to him saying, 'Whutis dis hoorisun?'

A lengthy explanation followed in broken English, describing the union of the earth and sky, but it only brought back the response, 'Whutis dis urt?' Several other instructors tried their hand, or rather their tongue, unsuccessfully and then Zulliman was packed off to the Royal Army Education Corps' emporium of learning at Beaconsfield for a six months' course in English. This, of course, could not have suited Yussif better as it meant six months added to his stay—and that close to the fleshpots of London.

Time passed quickly and Zulliman returned to Wallop with a remarkable command of the English language, more of which seemed to have been gained in the seedier districts of Soho than in the classroom. At length a somewhat apprehensive instructor sent him off on his first proper solo. All went well on start up, and he duly called for taxi instructions and disappeared over the brow of the hill. About half an hour later an agitated voice came over the radio in Air Traffic Control: 'Dis is Charlie 10. My engine is making strange noises.'

Quickly rising to the emergency, the controller came back: 'OK Charlie One Zero, keep calm. Where are you?'

There was a short pause, and then an anguished voice cried out: 'Oh my God! It has stopped! It has utterly stopped!'

By this time there was a cluster of anxious traffickers round the microphone. 'Where are you Charlie One Zero? Zulliman—*tell me where you are!*'

'Oh, yes, Sah.' came the agitated reply, 'I am by the caravan.'

Running the engine at tick over, it had taken him so long to do his pre-take off checks and to pluck up the courage to go, that the poor engine plugs had all oiled up and the labouring engine had finally come to a juddering stop before he had even left the ground.

One sunny morning not long afterwards, a controller gazing absently out of his tower at the stream of Chipmunks going round and round doing circuits and bumps, was alarmed to see one aircraft going along the downwind leg in the opposite direction to all the rest. Quick as a flash he snatched up his binoculars, read its side letter and came up on the radio: 'Chipmunk Charlie One Zero! You are going the wrong way round the circuit.'

This had singularly little effect, nor did a repeat fare any better. Exasperated and anxious, he called out in imperative tones: *'Chipmunk Charlie One Zero! Chipmunk Charlie One Zero! Who is the pilot in Chipmunk Charlie One Zero?'*

To which came back the phlegmatic reply: 'Dis is Chipmunk Charlie One Zero. Der is no pilot—only me!'

Once onto the next stage of his training, Intermediate Flight, and now flying Auster VIs, Zulliman was required to venture further afield and to find his way around the countryside by map reading. This was done by sending students round a series of navigation exercises which required them to check in by radio at the various turning points. Suspicion aroused by the fact that Zulliman was permanently lost when flying dual but appeared to have no difficulty when solo, his instructor sent him off on a map reading exercise and then followed in another aircraft. He did not have far to go. Just off the southern boundary of the airfield is the biggest, most conspicuous man-made tumulus in England, an Iron Age fort named Danebury Hill which had a distinctive, round clump of tall beech trees on its summit. Zulliman took off and made for this like a bee for a honey pot. Once there he went into orbit round it for the next hour, punctuating the time with regular calls on the radio to the effect that Charlie 10 was at point 1, 2 and so on. Having made the appropriate number of calls, he landed, reported a successful sortie and retired to the crewroom well satisfied with his efforts.

His instructor's remonstration with him over this minor peccadillo amazed Zulliman. (Apart from anything else—how did he know?) It also catapulted Zulliman into his next emergency—he left the circuit solo and got utterly lost. Various faint cries for help were heard from him from around the Home Counties and the controller responded to them by giving him bearings to steer for home. Eventually, alarmed by the length of time he had been airborne, the controller asked, 'Charlie One Zero, what is your endurance?' To which a faint voice came over the ether in reply: 'Endurance? Oh, endurance! It is Sun Life of Canada, I tink.'

Eventually, no thanks to the expensive Christmas presents he pressed on the Commandant and his family, Zulliman passed out—you remember the War Office mandate, oh my best beloved! A specially made pair of wings, not British Army pattern, were pinned to his chest and he returned to his native land leaving behind him a void which was difficult to fill.

Sadly, this is not the end of this little tale. Back home, Zulliman reported to the capital where the Royal Flight Anson stood on the dispersal awaiting an air test after some trifling repair. 'You are a pilot', said the Commander, 'Air test it!' On his mettle, or perhaps cowed by authority, Zulliman climbed aboard. By some miracle of mischance he managed to start not just one, but both engines —you may remember the Auster only has one—and, by an even more unkind quirk of fate, to taxi it onto the runway, but there his luck ran out. The aged,

LEAPING AND BOUNDING ACROSS THE DESERT WITHOUT LEAVING THE GROUND

44

Royal Anson trundled down the length of the runway and over the end of it without ever leaving the ground. It disappeared, bouncing and bounding across the desert in a cloud of dust, before eventually upending itself in a sand dune about a mile away.

Poor Yussif had met his Waterloo. His Majesty the King was not amused at the destruction of the Royal Flight and threw him into jail. For all I know he may still be there or, looking on the brighter side, came the revolution and he may now be the Chief of Air Staff.

## YUSSIF BIN ZULLIMAN

## HAD MET HIS WATERLOO

*For those of you who may read this, and who intend to embark on a career in Army Aviation—sit down in some quiet corner, take off your mittens and your shoes and socks and carefully count all your thumbs, fingers and toes.*

*If you do not come up with a grand total of 20, or even two lots of 10, remember Zulliman and re-direct your obvious talents elsewhere. It could prove a lot less painful for everyone.*

# CRASH BANG WALLOP

A prang, oh my best beloved, is an onomatopoeic term much loved by an older, moustachioed generation of RAF pilots. It graphically described a crash in which nobody got hurt, and Middle Wallop has had its fair share of them. Middle Wallop (Wallop derives from Vale Op, or Valley of the stream) acquired its unusual name long before aeroplanes even flew, let alone crashed on its hallowed ground but it was most appropriately named. Many and varied are the aircraft that have spread their vital parts over and around its confines in less than serious circumstances, since it first became an RAF airfield in 1940, then a Naval one and finally fell into Army hands in 1958. That aside, possibly some of the most interesting prangs there have been perpetrated by the Army.

An earlier one concerned an Auster, an Oxford and the crash tender. Prior to doing a standard forced landing practice on the airfield, the student in the Auster inadvertently put his finger on the transmit button while reciting a copybook Mayday call to his instructor, the august and ageless Jinx Jenks. On hearing the nerve-tingling word 'Mayday', the controller in the tower smashed his hand down on the crash alarm button, alerting the crash tender which then erupted out of its garage, lights flashing and bells ringing—and tore off across the airfield to the rescue.

Meanwhile, the Oxford (an ancient and revered twin engined machine left behind by the RAF) was doing circuits and bumps in the hands of an infanteer when an engine failed. Unfortunately it was the one which powered the hydraulic system, thus leaving the crew to pump down the wheels and the flaps by hand. Prolonged and vigorous pumping by the co-pilot, a gangling Gunner Lieutenant named Crutchley, finally persuaded both flaps to come down but only one wheel. By this time they were very late on finals.

The pilot, in the best traditions of the Infantry, decided to overshoot at the last minute but forgot, or never knew, that the Oxford was incapable of climbing, let alone overshooting, in that configuration. The exhausted Crutchley flung himself back at the pump again in a futile attempt to reverse the slow and laborious process, but to no avail. They touched, then skated, bounced and cartwheeled across the airfield and through somebody's garden before finally coming to rest against the back wall of the Wallop Post Office.

This was all too much for the eager crash tender crew. Having scented action (and fame at last) after weeks of boring inactivity interspersed with practices, they had the bit firmly between their teeth and were tearing across the airfield — like the charge of some mad Dervish—towards the Auster, when they saw the Oxford make its undignified exit through the hedge. Torn like a donkey between two carrots, the tender wobbled a few times on its breakneck path and then rolled over spectacularly in its indecision, scattering firemen in all directions.

Jenks and his student, partially if unwittingly to blame for the whole affair, found themselves confronted with the wreckage and got out to minister to their unfortunate would be rescuers—including one with a broken leg. Meanwhile the crew of the Oxford extracted themselves from their wreckage unaided. They went into the Post office and sent off a picture postcard to the CFI, before accepting consoling cups of tea from the patron and eventually walking home for supper.

Like them, oh my best beloved, always remember to report an accident or incident at the earliest possible opportunity.

In the early days of helicopter flying training it was customary, as a confidence booster, to send the student solo in the hover as soon as possible on his course. One sunny but breezy summer afternoon, an instructor famed for his suave, polished style rather more than his athletic prowess, climbed out of his Skeeter in the middle of the airfield and sent his latest student off on his first, observed solo hover.

With one lesson behind him, the student lifted off somewhat shakily and immediately began to drift towards his watching instructor. The latter stood his ground, mouthing and miming instructions, as long as he was able, but was eventually obliged to dodge out of the way for fear of being run down. At first he walked sheepishly along beside the machine discreetly gesticulating at the student inside, but to no avail. Faster and faster went the Skeeter and the instructor correspondingly quickened his pace and his gestures. Eventually, all dignity thrown to the wind, he was last seen sprinting across the airfield in hot pursuit of the errant aviator before the whole shooting match fetched up in a tangled heap in the hedge. The student climbed out of the wreckage and rounded accusingly on his wheezing and dishevelled instructor with 'You never showed me how to stop it!'

Attack, so they say, oh my best beloved, is the best form of defence.

Another spectacular incident was the crash of the pilotless Skeeter. In those days solo student pilots used to change over in the obvious and quickest way—the first pilot would land, latch down the controls, climb out and help the second to take his place. The whole business took but a minute before the aircraft was on its way again.

On this occasion the aircraft had landed between two hangers outside the OC's office. The first pilot was standing holding the door open for his successor, who was approaching under the disc, when the aircraft hopped up and down a few times and then lifted off altogether. The first pilot threw himself back in through the aircraft door and ended up lying face down across the seats, while the second flung himself flat on the ground with his hands over his head—and sustained severe gravel rash on his knees, elbows and nose in the process.

The Skeeter described a graceful arc through the air and then beat itself to death on the tarmac scattering bits of balsa wood, linen and scrap iron in all directions. The whole event was watched with interest by the OC standing at his window—that is until a metal plug from the end of a blade spar passed through the glass like butter, parted his hair and imbedded itself like a bullet in the wall behind him. Then he too took cover.

Perhaps, after all, the honours do go to the RAF. An RAF pilot was demonstrating a Single Pioneer to the Army as possible customers. The whole of Wallop—Director Land/Air Warfare, Brigadier Army Air Corps, staff, instructors, students and all had gathered alongside the tower to watch this professional display. He put it through its paces with style and flare, wheeling and bending it in front of the crowd.

His final *pièce de résistance* was a very low, very slow flypast. Unfortunately, in a moment of exuberance, he took both hands off the controls and turned and waved them at the open door, so that all could see just how stable the machine was. The aircraft responded instantly by falling out of the sky like a brick. It landed in a heap at General Pat Weston's feet amid rousing cheers from the admiring audience. As an encore, and to deafening applause, the red faced pilot crept out of the wreckage, saluted and disappeared into the crowd, never to be seen again.

No—surely honours must go to the Army. Rank hath its privileges. One clear, starlit night when the Auster VIIs of Intermediate Flight were night flying, the then Brigadier Army Air Corps decided to join in. He took off successfully in his turn, turned crosswind, down wind, onto base leg; and then set himself up on finals

for the faint glow of the crossed Landrover headlights below him. On the ground another student was cleared and taxied onto the take off point.

You have guessed it, oh my best beloved. Neither frantic radio calls nor red Very cartridges fired almost through his windscreen would deter him—the Brigadier was a man of decision and determination and had not reached his eminent rank and position by shilly-shallying. He landed firmly on the back of the Auster below, and there the two aircraft remained, as if locked in blissful copulation, for all to see in the morning.

The Brigadier was pleased, if a little surprised, by the shortness of his landing run. He was totally unaware that his engine had stopped as the propellor chewed its way up the back of the aircraft beneath to within an inch of its pilot's head, and that what he could hear was in fact the other engine throbbing underneath him. Stepping out of the aircraft to acknowledge the acclaim of the admiring throng rushing towards him out of the darkness, he fell six feet and sprained his shoulder.

An old and revered aviator named Warby once issued a blue instrument-rating card. It was directed towards deskbound, senior officers yearning to get back into the air. It had two holes in it to look through. The instructions on it read, 'Look through the holes at the sky. If the sky matches the card you may fly, otherwise on no account attempt anything so foolish' or words to that effect. Clearly the night sky did not match his card! In his enthusiasm, the Brigadier had exceeded the limitations of his blue instrument rating.

*Be sure, oh my best beloved, that however senior or junior you are, you never do the same.*

# THERE'S MANY A SLIP 'TWIXT CUP AND LIP

It seems hard to believe that the Scout was flying before many of you were born, oh my best beloved, and I with it. In the mid 1960s there was a minor war going on in Aden that reminded one of the North West Frontier in India and in 1966 the command of 24 Brigade, based at Falaise in Little Aden, changed hands.

A minor war going on in Aden: a close shave in a Scout

The final fling of the departing commander was a large luncheon party to be held in his quarter. The officers' quarters in Little Aden were set as an oval in the desert at the end of military habitation. The Brigadier's house was at the entrance to this elite little encampment. Like the others it had a small desert garden, which flourished with the addition of a little water. The garden was surrounded by an openwork purdah wall. Outside the wall, thriving on the fringes of moisture, a thick carpet of morning glory creeper, known as Camel's Foot, stretched for about ten yards before petering out in the sand beyond.

I, the Flight Commander, had been detailed to fly his guest of honour, the Commander in Chief, from his headquarters across the bay in Aden to the front door. As I approached I saw the Brigadier and his wife waiting to greet their guest, flanked by a crowd of officers' wives and hordes of children, who had all turned out to see the helicopter and the great man arrive. I set myself up for a smooth gentle approach to set down just in front of them.

I really should have known better, oh my best beloved but by the time I remembered, it was too late. As I neared the ground, the desert with all its filth and litter came up to meet us in a whirling storm. Women staggered backwards clutching flimsy tropical dresses about them, not knowing whether to preserve their eyes or their modesty. Children screamed and morning glory rolled itself up like a sprung carpet against the bottom of the wall.

Inside the aircraft it was just as bad. We flew without doors and I could hardly see the Commander in Chief beside me. At last the blades stopped, the dust cloud drifted away from the house and the awful scene was revealed. The ladies looked like survivors from a wreck. The brigadier's wife, a handsome woman, stood revealing more than she decently should. Her hairdo was an utter ruin matted with dust and debris. The Brigadier stepped forward to greet his guest and they shook hands, looking for all the world like two military ghosts meeting on the scene of a recent battle. The dust fell off them in clouds as they walked into the house together.

A sensible man, oh my best beloved, would have left the machine where it was and walked home. After all, I only lived next door. I started up, however, and took off to return to base, repeating the whole awful business. Looking back over my shoulder I knew that my days were numbered. The whole house had disappeared in a cloud of yellow horror.

That was not the least of the sorry affair. The house had evidently been thoroughly cleaned ready for handover the next morning. All the windows had been left open and lunch was a buffet affair laid out in the garden.

The new man immediately set about touring his scattered units. Some were in the Aden area; the rest were spread along the border with the Yemen between

Dhala in the West, Makeiras on the high plateau in the centre and Ataq on the edge of the Empty Quarter to the East. The main operational area was in the jebels to the North West (incorrectly called the Radfan) around Thumir (Habilayn) and Dhala. His units on a rotational basis permanently garrisoned both places.

When the new Brigadier arrived in Habilayn, 45 Commando Royal Marines were the resident battalion and my Flight (8 Flight) the resident Army Air Corps unit. The Marines (living up to their macho image) had arranged to take the poor man out on a patrol of awesome distance and rigour. Only too aware of his white knees and somewhat soft midriff, he made hasty arrangements with me to intercept the patrol, not too far from home, and whisk him away to an urgent engagement. I watched him depart at dawn in the middle of a line of craggy looking Marines who were clearly set on scaling every height and nourishing themselves en route with raw goat meat and lizards caught among the rocks. He looked for all the world like a biblical figure on the way to crucifixion.

He had previously noticed the two fixed forward firing machine guns mounted on a Scout and we had arranged that I would demonstrate them in action after I had rescued him. The guns were two General Purpose Machine Guns, mounted on the skids on either side of the fuselage and fired by a button on the pilot's cyclic stick. Sighting was somewhat rudimentary and consisted of a chinagraph pencil mark on the windscreen at an appropriate height. The ammunition belts were loaded with one-in-three tracer to indicate the fall of the shot. Rudimentary indeed, but highly effective; the guns accounted for more than one dissident on operations.

I duly arrived at the rendezvous and found him sitting on a rock, white, wheezing and dishevelled. He climbed in beside me and, grinning, said 'Thank God you've come. I'd just about had it!'

Leaving the macho Marines bounding like lions up the mountainside with belts of ammunition hanging round their necks and bleeding goat entrails dangling from the corners of their mouths, we flew off to the area which acted as a range. A wadi ran from North to South near the Eastern edge of the camp and airstrip. Beyond it a flat, rock-strewn plain sloped gently up to the foot of the jagged jebels two miles away. The plain was itself divided by a number of tributaries which ran from the hills to the main wadi nearby. This was the range area. Every evening, just before sundown, a hail of shot and shell crackled and crashed across it at Happy Hour—when all the camp defences tested their weapons and practised their musketry.

We circled the area to make sure that the range was clear. I selected a target of what appeared to be a litter of old 44-gallon drums. I pointed them out to the Brigadier as representing a gang of marauding dissidents, which we would engage tactically.

I turned away, dropped into the wadi and screamed up the valley, wheeling and bending around the corners. The poor Brigadier was already at a low ebb from his walk and I noticed that what little strength he had left in his legs was fast being spent bracing his feet against the floorboards. His knuckles were white as he gripped his Black Mafia cane across his chest; his teeth were clamped together and sealed by stretched dry lips—I wasn't called 'Low-Level Greville' for nothing! A sharp bend into one of the tributaries, which I knew led towards the target, and then I pulled up over the edge. There, smack in the middle of my chinagraph sight, were the drums.

I stabbed my thumb hard on the firing button. The guns chattered, the airframe shook and streams of tracer ripped towards the drums stitching clouds of dust around them.

To my horror the 'drums' all leapt to their feet and ran like demented scarecrows, leaping and jumping in all directions. My 'drums' had become a herd of goats tended by boys from the village.

My thumb froze on the button in horror as I zoomed overhead, still spitting fire. We turned back, our hearts in our mouths, expecting to find a scene of awful carnage. The Brigadier had gone grey and his previous tension had evaporated with the hint of a sag. He could clearly see a promising career ending with a political maelstrom in the first weeks of his new command. We arrived back at the scene and there was nothing there—nothing but the barren rocks of Aden and a litter of old 44-gallon drums.

Aden was a strange place. News travelled fast without help from telephone or jungle drums and we usually knew the result of our sporadic actions against the opposition the same day. We knew exactly who had been killed, who had been injured, how many and how badly. By the time we got back and landed, there was already much laughter in the village. 'Inshallah', the will of God, or divine justice had played a part. The boys, ignoring parental instructions, had taken the herd to graze nearer home in the 'Forbidden Place'. No sooner had they settled down than a screaming banshee had risen out of the ground beside them and the wrath of Allah had descended among them. Not a hair on their head nor, more to the point, on any of their goats had been harmed.

The Brigadier carried on his illustrious career and ended up as a General, but sadly, oh my best beloved, both he and others, if for different reasons, cast jaundiced eyes on the armed Scout thereafter.

*Be aware, oh my best beloved, that even in the most humble position, your actions can affect the course of history. Only now are we re-entering the era of the attack helicopter.*

# WHEN YOUR FEET TOUCH THE GROUND

You should be aware, oh my best beloved, if you have not discovered it already, that a career in Army Aviation is not all drifting around the ether wearing a noddy suit, white kid gloves, a big watch and a space helmet with the dark visor down. There are occasions when you must descend from the clouds, don working dress and soil or ink your fingers. This may be for a day, a month or even for a whole tour.

It came as a nasty shock when I found myself posted as Second in Command of an Aviation regiment in Germany. Having always commanded something throughout my service, whether platoon, flight or squadron, the transition from Chief (however minor) to Indian (however major) did not come easily. Added to that, my entire experience of BAOR amounted to a year as an infantry subaltern, commanding the Mortar Platoon of the Buffs, and a period when (still an infanteer) I was sent to form a Sapper Air Troop on integration trials. On the same trial, they had also managed to send another infanteer to form a Gunner Air Troop, plus a Sapper and a Gunner to an Infantry Air Platoon—a more inappropriate combination few other organisations could achieve. Neither of these two episodes had given me much insight into managing the divisional battle in the British Army of The Rhine.

Having been brought up in the days of the Brigade Air Squadron and Regimental Flights the whole concept of the Aviation Regiment was new and anathema to me. I arrived to find a Regimental Headquarters in the middle of a Divisional Headquarters and not an aeroplane in sight. The three squadrons were spread over the length and breadth of North Germany, doing their own thing and studiously ignoring the management and the firm next door. Old habits die hard and the 'old dog' was far from dead.

I must have been as much of a trial to my new Commanding Officer as he was to me, for I was as ignorant and inept as he was pompous and humourless. The combination had fathomless possibilities. My morale and self-esteem suffered a further blow when I found myself sharing an office with the Adjutant, a singularly erudite and intelligent young man who knew more about everything than I could ever hope to, and who was clearly destined for high places. His knowledge of things military was boundless. He knew every detail of the Division and Corps function and every organisation and weapon in the Red Army. He could write a regimental operation instruction, complete with complicated signals plan, while discussing a forthcoming function over the telephone, in fluent German, with the local Burgermeister.

The first divisional exercise I attended only proved my ineptitude. The Air Cell, consisting of our Regimental HQ and the Divisional Air Liaison Officer or DALO, shared a box body command post truck or, to be more precise, two of them, which leapfrogged each other from place to place as we moved. They were filled with an assortment of radios which hissed and screamed simultaneously, a vast map of an unfamiliar area covered in unintelligible hieroglyphics, and a crank-handle field telephone. The latter was backed by an operations chart reminiscent of an ancient family tree and defied any efforts I made to communicate with anybody. The Adjutant managed all this with consummate ease, while simultaneously writing the operational instruction for the next Divisional Ski Meeting—but to me each spell on watch was an ordeal which I approached with dread and foreboding. The CO would sit, silent, aloof and disapproving, in his canvas camp chair in the corner of the cell with cold, unsympathetic eyes boring into the back of my sweating neck as I fumbled my way from one disaster to the next.

The exercise culminated in an NBC strike. It came, inevitably, while I was on watch. Harsh rattles in the pre-dawn darkness sounded, warning of gas attack. In a trice the CO and DALO had donned their suits and their gas masks and became unrecognisable, unfriendly, shapeless monsters. I, meanwhile, whipped out the first of my plastic packets. Being a smart regimental officer and new to the game, I had always wondered why everyone in the headquarters carried their NBC suits in huge shapeless bundles tied up with string, like so many itinerant refugees. Mine took up far less space and looked so much smarter in its vacuum-packed plastic packets neatly stowed in a square canvas haversack.

It took some considerable time to tear open the thick plastic wrapping. The telephone buzzed and I reached for it with one hand as I impatiently shook out the contents of the packet with the other. A solid, vacuum compressed block shot out across the room and caught the CO squarely in the solar plexus. A noise like a trick cushion erupted from the side of his gas mask and he collapsed backwards into his camp chair like a giant fly neatly swatted.

I retrieved my brick and tore it apart, breaking all my fingernails in the process. It turned out to be the smock—the trousers go on first. I opened the second packet, rather more carefully, and attacked the brick-like content with my dinner knife. I jabbed several nasty holes in it in the process, but eventually revealed a flat trouser shape that appeared to have been run over by a steamroller. I ripped the top apart and thrust one leg down into it until it finally stuck fast and would go no further. At the same time I pushed my head and shoulders into the equally flat smock. With a supreme effort my head eventually burst out at the top, but I ran out of strength with one arm pinioned half way down one sleeve and the other hand somewhere inside the smock, desperately scrabbling to find an opening into its sleeve.

SHRIEKED IN UNINTELLIGIBLE REPLY

The telephone rang and the radio crackled. I answered them both simultaneously, despite finding extreme difficulty in grasping the handsets or pressing the speech switch, or indeed in speaking at all as by now I was out of breath and in a muck sweat.

'Ha wa!' The noise came from behind me. I spun round clutching the squawking telephone in a shrouded fist. It came from the masked figure of the CO. I must have done him more damage than I thought.

'Ha wa!' he mumbled from within his gas mask. I looked at him inquiringly.

'Haa waa er gor!' he exploded angrily, repeatedly stabbing a rubber gloved finger first at my bare head and then at his own gas mask and gloved hand. With the flat, tightly stuck sleeves flapping from the ends of my hands, I dragged out my gas mask and pulled it over my head, firmly trapping one sleeve underneath it.

By now I was irreparably trussed up. Both feet were pinioned in sealed trouser legs with the crotch well below my knees. One arm was pinned to my head and the other was struggling wildly to escape from its sleeve. Worse, I was completely blind! The inside of my gas mask had steamed up.

The telephone squawked angrily, both radios burst into furious life simultaneously and I shrieked back at them unintelligibly through my gas mask in reply. At that moment the door opened behind me and struck me a smart blow in the small of the back. I staggered across the room and then pitched forward on my face in a heap, dragging down telephones and headsets with me. By now, inexcusably, I had lost my rag.

'*Efforf you bloody idiot!*' I yelled into my steaming mouthpiece. Thinking it was the incomparable Adjutant being playful, I dragged off my gas mask and turned round to give him the rest with both barrels, only in more lucid tones.

It was the Divisional Commander.

Back in the barracks things did not go much better. The Squadrons were very independent, safely distant and not towing the line to the CO's satisfaction, and I got the blame. Our office was next to the CO's with an inter-connecting door between the two, and I passed in and out of it like a yo-yo to receive his admonishment, until even the Adjutant gave me a brief look of sympathy.

One day I borrowed a mattress, some six-inch nails and a large hammer from the QM and nailed the mattress to the wall opposite the connecting door. The noise drew the CO's attention and mild curiosity. I explained that it was to make it less painful next time he threw me out of his office, but he neither smiled nor got the message.

Eventually the CO decided he must lay down the law—he would hold a conference and harangue all his officers. Like Lars Porsina of Clusium, he sent his messenger (me) East and West and North and South, to summon his array...and to make all the arrangements.

Now if there was one thing I thought I could do properly, it was to arrange a wretched conference. This one would be a shining example to all and would restore my good name. I had tables arranged in a huge U and bullied the Quartermaster into procuring miles of pristine green baize to cover them. There were printed nameplates on stands for everyone attending and a stack of fresh, lined paper and a new, sharpened pencil in each place. There were ashtrays in the places of all who smoked and a silver salver in the corner, loaded with glasses and decanters of sherry. Finally, there was my *pièce de résistance*—a rostrum at the head of the U, and on it a brand new lectern faced with the regimental crest. The whole effect was most impressive and rather like the United Nations General Assembly.

The day dawned, the minions gathered, drank their sherry and took their places. I personally occupied a servile place at the back of the room near the door. Precisely at 10 o'clock the RSM, well briefed by me, called 'Gentlemen!' and discreetly withdrew as the Great Man appeared in the doorway. The room stood in respect and awe as he strode the length of it and mounted the rostrum. Steely-eyed, he looked slowly round the gathering, quelling them with his personality. A deathly hush descended and he opened his mouth to speak.

At this precise moment, some gnome somewhere in the building decided to attack the central heating pipes with an electric drill. The sound rattled and echoed round the room like an empty 44-gallon drum being massaged with a road drill. The CO's mouth shut and his eyes swivelled round to me in furious, silent indignation and accusation. The noise stopped—he tried again and the same thing happened. Again his eyes settled coldly on me. I raised a forefinger and nodded in acknowledgement, letting him know that all would soon be well. I got to my feet, went to the door, turned the handle and pushed. Unfortunately the door opened inwards. There was a sharp crack, a dull rumbling and the whole door, frame and all, fell out into the corridor with a splintering crash.

LOOKED BACK THROUGH THE DUST

Shaken but putting a brave face on it, I climbed over the debris and looked back through the dust at the open mouthed, stunned faces beyond.

The drill was grinding even louder out there in the corridor and, in a dull, pathetic attempt to keep the noise from interrupting the CO further, I bent down, grasped the top of the door frame in both hands, lifted it up and rammed it firmly back into place.

In my misery, I heard the whole room erupt into howls of uncontrollable laughter as I fled.

*Strange things happen, oh my best beloved, so never despair, however black the picture... Shortly after that I was promoted and went to warmer climes. I never did discover whether the confidential report that secured that promotion was written in appreciation or desperation.*

# PRACTICE MAKES PERFECT

There are those innocents who soldier under the delusion that an exercise is the time for making mistakes with impunity that one would not wish to make in battle. Be aware, oh my best beloved, that nothing could be further from the truth. Many's the promising military career that has sunk into the mud of Salisbury Plain, crumbled in the dust of Sennelager Ranges, or been trampled under the feet of one marching to Whitehall by way of Sennybridge. Of course you must also see things from the other fellow's point of view. Many's the blossoming career that has been withered by the blundering incompetence of some lesser mortal under command.

As a subaltern, commanding the three-inch mortar platoon, I had a National Service ensign as my second in command. He was a fully qualified barrister, somewhat older than myself, who answered to the name of Oublie. Oublie was pear-shaped and bore a strong resemblance to Quasimodo, but he was one of the nicest of God's chosen people that I have ever known. That said, he was a shambling military disaster and he was my cross in life. Physically he was totally uncoordinated and, worse, anything he touched fell apart in his hands. His turnout reduced the RSM to apoplexy. Even five minutes after his batman's most devoted ministrations, and the combined efforts of the rest of the platoon (who all adored him), he looked like a sack of potatoes that had been dunked in a sheep dip. In the courts martial room, once the shock of his appearance had worn off, he was awesome—but even the simplest military task was a disaster in his hands.

Only he could put a mortar bomb down the barrel upside down in the middle of a major demonstration—causing the rapid departure of spectators and demonstrators alike; or, on a cod night live-firing exercise, get the whole platoon totally inebriated in their mortar pits to devastating effect, by hopelessly miscalculating the rum ration; or yet again—perhaps his '*pièce de résistance*'— wrecking a major film in which the Battalion was involved by leading the whole platoon (eight vehicles in line abreast) like the charge of the Light Brigade at full gallop into a swamp, with cameras whirring and clacker boards clacking. The heroine, a professional actress, had hysterics. The hero, a somewhat precious long-haired actor, went off in a sulk, and it took a week to recover the vehicles and the cast to shoot the scene again.

This was an exercise but I have seen roughly the same thing happen in anger. One evening in Kenya, during the Mau Mau emergency, I was innocently supping my half pint of Tusker in the bar of Barry's Hotel, Thompsons Falls, when a figure came in wearing a working safari suit and buckskin chaps, carrying a minor arsenal around his person. He flipped his bush hat on to the bar, crashed a Sten gun down beside it and added two Smith and Wesson six shooters from their tooled leather hip holsters. Finally, hefting two 36 Grenades out of his belt and dropping them noisily on the pile, he growled 'Whisky!' to the unimpressed African barman. The figure turned out to be a member of the Kenya Police Mounted Reserve.

The Kenya Police Mounted Reserve was a special force raised for the emergency. Mounted on horseback and aided by trackers, its role was to arrive on the scene of an incident and swiftly follow up a gang over rough country. Carried away by their name and their role, they looked for all the world like a posse out after Billy the Kid.

One day they came over the brow of a hill and hit on a large gang below them, busy chopping up the inhabitants of a village and hamstringing their cattle and stock. The leader of the posse waved his men into extended line along the crest and then, sounding the charge, thundered down the slope at full gallop, himself in the lead. The gang broke and ran but the gap between them narrowed quickly. As it finally closed, the leader raised his Sten gun and opened fire. His first shot took his horse straight behind the ears and it crashed pole-axed into the dust, bringing half the rest of the patrol down with it.

Perhaps, oh my best beloved, if, like Oublie's charge, it had first happened in practice, all might have been well on the day.

Once, tasked with conducting a tactical night move of the whole battalion, I foolishly gave Oublie the map and put him in the front vehicle to lead the way, while I positioned myself somewhere near the middle of the convoy the better to control the unwieldy affair. We trundled through the rain without lights in the inky darkness, nose to tail, following the feeble glow of the convoy light ahead. Suddenly the truck ahead stopped so quickly that we almost rode up its rear, and I felt a jolt as the truck behind failed to stop in time. I sat there for a while, waiting to move on again, when I became aware that we were on a cross track and there was a vehicle on my left waiting to cross. I climbed out, went over to it and looked in through the window. There, to my horror, I saw the freely perspiring Oublie desperately scrabbling through a litter of crumpled soggy maps, utterly lost.

The dank and dripping dawn eventually broke and revealed the awful scene. The whole convoy lay locked nose-to-tail in an enormous, immovable loop like some snake trying to swallow its own tail. '*Mr Edgecombe to the Commanding Officer*' —the cry was passed gleefully down the line. I climbed despondently on to a motorcycle, kicked it into life and set off, preparing yet another limp explanation as I went.

On a bend in the track, standing in the mist and drizzle under a group of gnarled firs the other side of a large puddle of water, I came across a little tableau for all the world like some demonic reception party on the banks of the River Styx. It consisted of the Commanding Officer, his Adjutant, the RSM, my Company Commander and, worse, the Brigade Commander—all standing in dreadful stony silence awaiting my arrival. I steeled myself and rode slowly through the puddle towards them, ready for the worst.

THE PUDDLE GOT DEEPER AND DEEPER

Imagine the scene, oh my best beloved: the might of authority arrayed in front of me and a sea of grinning faces in an endless chain of interlocked vehicles behind. I wished the ground would open up and swallow me—*it did!* As I rode forward, the puddle grew inexorably deeper and deeper and I sank slowly up to my armpits before the engine finally stalled underneath me with a sucking, gurgling noise. I sat to attention on my by now totally submerged machine, saluted as smartly as I could under the circumstances and said, 'Sir, you sent for me?

If you're going to make a foul up, oh my best beloved, and no doubt some day you will, it helps to create a diversion which raises a smile and puts your crime into perspective.

Realism in training is something to be striven after, but not at any cost. By chance I had the first Army pilot State Registered Nurse as a student. One day, wending our way down the low level route past Bulford to the ranges, we actually watched a car crash head-on into a telegraph pole. Seizing the opportunity for realism, I told him to land beside it and sort it out—which he did with élan, efficiency and enthusiasm. Hardly had the dust and smoke subsided before an unconscious, bleeding figure had been extracted from the wreckage, expertly patched up and loaded into an ambulance which we had called to the scene by radio. We went on our way smugly congratulating ourselves on our efficiency and our contribution to public relations. Unfortunately the victim's first words on waking up in hospital were 'I looked up and saw a helicopter coming down the road towards me—and then I woke up here.'

The search for ealism in training can lead to some bizarre situations. I once had to support a School of Infantry exercise on Salisbury Plain with a Skeeter. I was to join the exercise for the final advance phase, after attending the Battalion 'O' Group the night before. To add realism, I decided to fly to join the 'O' Group as if I had just been called in by radio. The flight direct would be very brief so I planned to do it in three legs, as if going to Beachy Head by way of Bannockburn.

Night fell and with it a gentle drizzle as I took off into the darkness. Now whether the wind was not quite as forecast or my calculation were not all they might have been, when my allotted time was up there was nothing (let alone a grid reference) in the middle of Salisbury Plain, that I even faintly recognised. I droned round in ever increasing circles, searching for anything that would give me a clue. Finally, in desperation, I decided to land and ask—or at least to find a known start point. Heading out of the blackness towards the nearest habitation, I found an open square surrounded by lights and landed thankfully. I was just lighting a nerve-soothing cigarette, when a heavy hand fell on my shoulder and a firm voice said 'I think you'd better come along with me!' and I found myself locked behind bars.

I had landed on the secure, nuclear square at Larkhill!

My arrival was like manna from heaven to the bored security police and, with stubborn but puckish humour, they relished every moment of it. I had no means of identification on me and they were not going to 'let me go' till I proved myself. In a moment of folly I suggested that they ring up the Mess at Wallop where a friend would vouch for me. They did and he didn't. It was after midnight and I had forgotten there was a dinner on that night. A slurred voice said, 'Never heard of him' and its owner put the phone down. I never did make the 'O' group, nor the dawn attack for that matter, but the bacon, eggs and coffee, admirably served in my cell the next morning, were well worth the rub.

*Play it for real, oh my best beloved, but never lose your sense of humour or we are all lost.*

# THE FINGER OF FATE

You, oh my best beloved, may possibly have got the impression from previous Tales For Beginners that I am alone in getting both feet in the mire — there have been times when I have thought so myself. Let me assure you that this is not the case. After a minor incident on one of Her Majesty's sail training yachts, a kindly senior officer dropped me a letter (that was possibly pointed but more, I like to think, in consolation) that illustrates this point.

The incident? It occurred during a sail-training course—with three Generals and a Brigadier as student crew—when fate put her hand to the wheel. Overcome by the seniority (far be it for me to say the ham-fistedness) of her crew, the yacht's throttle linkage seized at 'full ahead' while manoeuvring into the Grove & Gutterage Marina amongst the mass of boats gathered there for Cowes Week. Cowes is the Mecca of sailing and this was its main religious festival. The scene that followed was traumatic to say the least and is etched indelibly on my memory.

'I have control' is probably the last thing one should say under such circumstances (better to retire below with a newspaper and a bottle of malt and let events take their course) but say it I did. Flinging myself at the helm, I aimed at a gap in the mass of boats alongside, meanwhile 'wracking' the throttle lever desperately to and fro. The crew, wearing distinctive navy blue sweaters with JSSC emblazoned across the chest—were smartly lining the side of the (unmistakably Army) red hull. They held coiled warps in their hands, waiting to step lightly ashore with them as we eased alongside.

Two things happened simultaneously: we hit the pontoon head on and I irrevocably hit reverse gear.

The crew was instantly reduced to two—a General and myself. The former was lying on his back on the galley floor with an upturned washing-up bowl plus all its greasy contents across his chest. The remaining three, moaning in pain, were strewn around the pontoon in ignominiously prone positions, at the feet of sailing's hierarchy, inextricably tangled in a web of rope.

There was no time to dawdle or sympathise as by now the boat was picking up speed backwards. I advised those ashore to make fast and then, letting go everything else, I dropped to the cockpit floor, feet braced against the bulkhead, and pulled desperately on an unresponsive engine decompression plug with both hands.

Have you ever watched the losing side in a tug-of-war match, oh my best beloved? Just as the engine (thankfully) stopped, I looked up over the side and saw three wheezing gentlemen in an extremis of exhaustion. Legs splayed apart, bodies arched backwards, teeth grimly clenched together and eyes out like organ stops, they were clinging to their ropes and being slowly and inexorably dragged across the pontoon. I regret to say that they lacked the moral fibre expected of their rank and service because, on reaching the edge, they all three let go.

Some time later after considerable confusion and loss of dignity, we were eventually tied up alongside safely.

You will appreciate that my morale was already at a low ebb when an official looking letter with a JSSC stamp on the back dropped onto my desk. To my surprise, its only content was a report to a company chairman by the master of a freighter caught in an incident somewhat similar to my own. It read:

Dear Sir

It is with regret and haste that I write this letter to you; regret that such a small misunderstanding could lead to the following circumstances, and haste in order that you will get this report before you form your own pre-conceived opinions from reports in the world press, for I am sure that they will tend to overdramatise the affair.

We had just picked up the pilot and the apprentice had returned from changing the 'G' flag to the 'H'. It being his first trip, he was having difficulty in rolling up the 'G' flag properly. I therefore proceeded to show him how. Taking hold of the corner, I told him to let go his end. The lad, though willing, is none too bright, necessitating my having to repeat the order in a sharper tone.

At this precise moment the Chief Officer appeared from the Chart Room, having been plotting the vessel's progress and, thinking that it was the anchors that I was referring to, relayed the order 'let go' to the Second Officer on the forecastle. The port anchor, having been cleared away but not walked out, was promptly let go. The effect of letting the anchor drop from the 'pipe' while the vessel was proceeding at full harbour speed proved too much for the windless brake and the entire length of the port cable was pulled out 'by the roots'. I fear that the damage in the chain locker may be extensive. The braking effect of the port anchor naturally caused the vessel to sheer violently in that direction — right towards a swing bridge that spans a tributary of the river up which we were proceeding.

The swing bridge operator showed great presence of mind by opening the bridge for my vessel. Unfortunately, he did not think to stop the vehicular traffic on it, with the result that the partially opened bridge deposited a Volkswagen, two cyclists and a cattle truck on the foredeck. My ship's company are at present engaged in rounding up the contents of the latter which, from the noise, I would say were pigs. In his efforts to arrest the progress of the vessel, the Second Officer dropped the starboard anchor but regrettably too late to be of any practical use, for it fell on the swing bridge operator's control cabin, and with him still inside.

After the port anchor was let go and the vessel started to sheer, I gave the ring for 'Full Astern' on the engine room telegraph and personally rang the engine room to order maximum astern revolutions. I was informed that the sea temperature was 53° and was asked if there was a film on that night—my reply would not add constructively to this report.

Up until now I have confined my report to the activities at the forward end of the vessel. Back aft, they were having their own problems.

At the moment the port anchor was let go, the Third Officer was supervising the making fast of the after tug having lowered the ship's towing spring down onto its deck. The sudden braking effect of the port anchor caused the tug to run in under the stern of my vessel—just at the moment when the propellors were answering my double ring for 'Full Astern'. The prompt action of the Third Officer in securing the inboard end of the towing spring delayed the sinking of the tug by some minutes, thereby allowing the safe abandonment of that vessel.

It is strange but, at the very moment of letting go the port anchor, there was a complete power cut ashore. The fact that we were passing over a 'cable area' at the time might suggest that we may have touched something on the river bed. The power cut was fortunate indeed as it meant that the high tension cables brought down across the foredeck by the foremast were not live. I regret that, owing to the blackout ashore, it was impossible to see where the pylons fell but they did so with considerable noise.

The actions and behaviour of foreigners during moments of minor crisis never fail to amaze me. The pilot, for instance, is, at this very moment, huddled in the corner of my day cabin, alternately crooning to himself and crying, having consumed a whole bottle of my gin in a time that is worthy of inclusion in the Guinness Book of Records. The tug captain, on the other hand, reacted violently and has had to be forcibly restrained by the steward, who now has him handcuffed in the ship's hospital, where he is telling me to do impossible things with my ship and my crew.

I enclose the names and addresses of the drivers and insurance companies of the vehicles on my foredeck, which the Second Officer managed to collect before his somewhat hurried evacuation of the forecastle. These particulars will enable you to claim for the damage the vehicles did to the railings of the No 1 hold.

I am closing this preliminary report now because I am finding it difficult to concentrate with the sound of police sirens and their flashing lights in my eyes.

It is sad to think that, had the apprentice appreciated that there was no need to fly pilot flags after dark, none of this need ever have happened.

Yours truly

Master

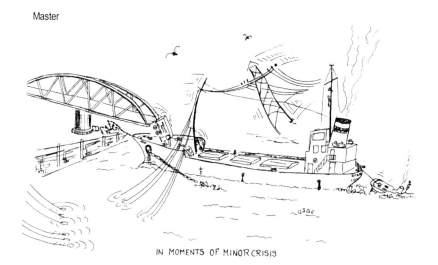

IN MOMENTS OF MINOR CRISIS

The point I make, among others, oh my best beloved, is that things do sometimes go wrong, even in the best of circles and despite every effort and precaution.

Be advised:

Do report things if they happen to you;

Do not be too quick to cry 'negligence' when it happens to others—there is such a thing as fate.

Even Nelson acknowledged this when, dying, he said 'Kismet (it is fate) Hardy'.

*Some people do indeed nudge fate against themselves by their own folly, but others are truly victims of fate and just make the best of a bad lot. In the latter case a cup of kindness may do more good all round than the hangman's noose.*

# KEEPING UP WITH THE JONESES

Old habits die hard but for your own peace of mind, oh my best beloved, it is often better to shrug off the old and keep abreast of changes.

You may remember that, some time ago, I warned you against dabbling in the other Services' mystiques. What I did not warn you about was the host of strange mystiques within your own service—and they far outdo anything the other Services can muster.

An SAS Officer, an Australian, was once called to London for a long briefing and, for the first time, was put up for the night in the Officers' Mess of the resident Guards Battalion in Chelsea Barracks. When he came down to breakfast the next morning, he was somewhat surprised to find the officer sitting opposite him at the table, lost in the Financial Times, was wearing a silk dressing gown and his enormous bearskin dress hat.

'Stringe people thaese Poms,' he thought as he shook out a generous helping of cornflakes onto his crested plate and sloshed milk over them from a beautiful Waterford crystal jug.

The sugar in its magnificent Georgian silver bowl, along with the heavy Regency silver salt cellar and pepper pot, the beautiful Crown Derby butter dish and a rather motley looking collection of sticky HP Sauce bottles, precariously balanced on a NAAFI saucer, were all clustered round the officer's place, just out of reach across the polished walnut table.

'Excuse me' he said, 'would you pahss the sugar?'

To his surprise there was absolutely no response whatsoever, so he tried again, a little louder; but still with the same result. Getting impatient, and wondering whether all Poms were deaf as well as strange, he raised his voice and shouted,

'Hi there—could you pahss the sugar, mite?'

At that, the only other person in the room, immersed in a copy of the Times, looked up and said mildly 'Do you mind! When a fellow wears his hat at the breakfast table, it means that he doesn't want to be spoken to. Sort of, *not there*, y'know.'

The Australian sat back stunned and then, in mounting fury, he pushed back his Regency chair, undid his boot laces, removed his boots, pulled off his socks and, hoisting both hairy, naked feet onto the table, he splashed them noisily and messily in his cornflakes.

At last the figure opposite him took notice and looked up. An expression of horrified disbelief came across his face.

'I say!' he said, appalled, 'what on earth are you doing?'

'Well mite,' was the rejoinder, 'Where oiy come frum, when a feller tikes his beuts off and flaps his kippers in his cornflikes, it means *pahss the bloody sugar!*'

There is, of course, a right and a wrong way of asking for anything. The Gunners in particular make something of a fetish of the niceties of requesting their support. On my flying course, it seemed as if I spent as much, if not more, time learning the Gunner mystique for calling for Artillery support as I did actually learning to fly. This took place in classrooms, kneeling under the puff range (where I first took up chain smoking cigarettes), in the radio room and, for interminable hours, in countless draughty bunkers around Salisbury Plain. All this was under the tutelage of what appeared to be Royal Artillery brigadiers who, I subsequently discovered, were in fact quite junior officers masquerading in red hatbands.

It all seemed a bit like the 'bearskin' to me—a trifle overdone, especially as I had just come from commanding an infantry three-inch mortar platoon, where the same thing all seemed so much simpler. At last I was drilled to their satisfaction and was ushered out into the wide, operational world, certified 'Gunner Acceptable'.

The years rolled by and there seemed to be little call for this particular skill until a long time later, when I got to Aden. There, Brigade HQ, not content with fighting a minor war up-country and an internal security situation in the urban areas, was out in the desert on exercise when I was summoned to an 'O' Group. Impressed by the urgency of the call, I leapt into a Scout and, in the gathering dusk, came to a screeching halt just outside the Brigade Command Post tent.

I hurried inside only to be confronted by a scene that stopped me dead in my tracks. The dim light of the field lighting set could hardly penetrate the clouds of dust and sand billowing around, and there was paper everywhere—plastered round the ceiling, wafting round the room and settling, with the dust, on the furniture, the floor and people's heads and shoulders like autumn leaves after a whirlwind. There was even one piece, with a long ink smear across it as if dragged from under a pen, being noisily shredded by the table fan mounted on the Brigadier's desk. It stood there blasting shreds of paper and a whirling stream of sand into the Brigadier's dust-covered face.

Be aware, oh my best beloved, of the chaos that your own downwash can create!

The Brigadier was a magnanimous man and, slit-eyed, spitting sand and shredded paper from pursed lips and fanning a hand in front of his face, he got straight to the point. The Yemenis had acquired a field piece which they had started loosing off across the border into Makeiras, a Gunner outpost in the mountains of the central area of the Aden/Yemen border. They did so around dawn every morning and no one could find where it was firing from, so they wanted an Air OP there the next morning to find it and sort it out. Spitting and picking at the last bit of paper stuck to his lip, the Brigadier said 'Be in the area of Grid Reference 1234 at dawn tomorrow. Find it, and deal with it!' Then, coughing theatrically, he added, 'Oh, and by the way, you might send some of your lads round to tidy up here after you've gone!'

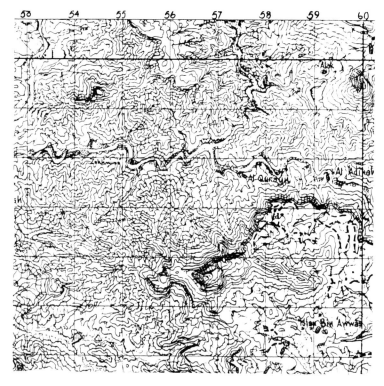

The hills did not match my black and white contour map

72

Tension mounted that night as I carefully planned my route. Finding the area in the dark was going to be tricky and, what's more, it was in the Upper Yaffa—bad, goolie-money country! For those uninitiated and innocent among you, oh my best beloved, goolie-money is used to keep certain portions of your anatomy housed where they are most useful, rather than having them sewn up in your mouth by the locals when you are caught.

At last I was ready and, pocketing my Wallop 'Point Engagement' crib, I set off in the darkness for my target some 90 miles away.

It was a beautiful dawn as, with 10,000 feet on the clock, I manoeuvred into as concealed a position as possible among the jebel tops near the border (after all, I didn't want to frighten them off). Across the border the rocky hills lay in a dark rich purple haze which somehow did not seem to match my black and white contour map. As I tried to dovetail one to the other, something caught my eye, and I looked up just in time to see a flash…that was no reflection, the sun wasn't up yet…and then a faint plume of smoke.

Excitement mounting, I scanned the map and fixed the spot, at the same time nudging my musty Wallop crib onto my kneepad—this was the real thing at last! Composing myself, I pressed the transmit button and, trying to quell the excitement tingeing my voice, put out that stirring call which all Gunners used to live for.

'Hullo One. This is Alpha Six One Alpha. *Target! Target! Target!* Over.'

The response could not have been more deflating. I would have done better had I taken off my boots and socks and dabbled my feet in my cornflakes. A calculatedly bored Horse Artillery voice from some sandbagged position below came back: 'Oh my Gawd, *here comes Pontius Pilate!*'

*Keep yourself up to date, Oh my best beloved. If nothing else it may preserve your ego and your dignity.*

*The Gun? Well, after what followed, it never fired again!*

# IF THE LORD HAD INTENDED ME TO FLY...

In days of yore, possibly before your time, Oh my best beloved, Wallop was the Mecca for anyone with bright ideas, high hopes and a home-made flying machine that they wanted to sell. The Army— still in the balloon era mentally, if not physically—was always interested in lookig over the next hill and was game to try anything.

One such machine answered to the pseudonym of the Durex Delta. Synonymous with a popular brand of rubber goods, the machine had about the same flying characteristics as its more famous namesake—slow to rise and limiting to all but the thrusting or safety conscious.

It consisted of a delta-shaped, rubber, inflatable wing section with an old-fashioned, square laundry basket on wheels suspended underneath it. The whole ensemble was driven not by steam, but by a small motorcycle engine attached to the back of the basket in pusher mode. It was controlled by a stick (literally a length of broomstick) suspended in front of the pilot from above, which worked in the opposite sense to the norm in other aircraft—you pushed to go up and pulled to go down. A child's pedal-car crank, powered by the engine, worked a set of fireside bellows built into the front of the wing and kept the contraption inflated. The effect, coming towards you with the pink bellows opening and closing in the sliver wing, was like a pond fish gulping for air. When not in use, the wing was deflated and the whole ensemble, engine and all, was packed away in the laundry basket.

A seemingly more unlikely pilot would have been difficult to find than the one selected to trial this machine. He was a tall, elegant cavalryman of impeccable breeding and manner, with a penchant for horses and cherry-coloured trousers. Indeed it may well have been his skill on the hunting field that influenced the decision. He flew the thing with great verve and élan, if such was possible. Strangely enough he never crashed it, despite the fact that it took the entire length of the airfield to get airborne, seldom rose above twenty feet, and was about as

manoeuverable as a flying dishcloth. He lived to further amaze students of the military selection system when, being a fluent Turkish linguist, he was selected to be the Military Attaché in (Arabic) Khartoum.

In those days the ground school was isolated in Seco huts, long since demolished, over the brow of the hill on the south side of the airfield. Dull lectures on photography and Met were occasionally enlivened by the sight of incompetent students trying to land an Auster in the 'Box' painted on the short landing strip outside the window. One could sometimes get a lift home across the airfield on the salvage vehicle that came out to collect the remains. None of this prepared us for the first flight of the Durex Delta.

The first indication of something unusual was a distant sound, like continuously tearing canvas; bored eyes were drawn to the window. The noise gradually increased in volume before its extraordinary source crested the hill and lumbered down the slope towards us. At first we thought it was a joke as, with huge bloated wing weaving and pulsating, orange mouth gulping, the basket jiggling and bouncing underneath, it wobbled slowly and unsteadily towards us. Then, to our amazement, it took to the air—but only just—and headed straight for us, some six feet off the ground.

By this time, lesson forgotten, we were all at the window cheering the monster on. The sudden realisation that it might not clear the hut had everyone flat on the

Randy and ready to go: Messrs Watts, Watton and Bandy

floor among the chalk dust and pencil sharpenings before, with a final desperate heave on the reins, it scraped over the roof. We all rushed for the opposite window. Danebury Hill, surprisingly, presented less of a problem as (though in his flight path) the pilot was just able to circumnavigate its base and make his way back to the comparative safety of the airfield. We never saw it fly again.

One of the more entertaining contenders for military stardom was the Wallis Benson Autogyro— a single-seater velocipede brought spectacularly to fame in one of the James Bnd films when, fitted with more hardware than a Harrier, it was brilliantly flown by its designer and maker.

Lured by its low cost and alive to its potential uses, ranging from aerial observation to airborne motorcycle despatch riders, the Army procured three of them for trial and evaluation. The idea was to see if complete novices could be taught to fly them with the minimum of training. It was decided to try them first on helicopter pilots, then fixed wing pilots and finally complete novices to flying. Sadly, or perhaps fortunately, the idea never caught on. Possibly there might have been more success if they had started with the less expert and worked upwards, but as it was the novice pilots between them crashed the entire fleet in fairly short order.

The machine consisted of a child's tricycle with a small pusher engine at the back and a freewheeling rotor on top. The pilots were selected more for their otiose nature and diminutive size and weight than for any particular skill. They donned every item of clothing they could find, topped it off with the old school muffler and leather rimmed Biggles goggles and reported for duty looking for all the world like miniature Michelin-tyre-men.

The first problem was how to teach them. To begin with there was not even an autogyro-qualified pilot around let alone an instructor or, for that matter, any instructions. Secondly the machine was very much a single-seater and lastly there was no radio or any other means of communication.

The first of these was overcome by issuing each intrepid aviator with a set of home-made pilot's notes. The remainder were addressed by the senior test officer, not adjudged an athlete even by his best friends, running, and later peddling a bicycle alongside—shouting instructions through a loud hailer, while the student performed a series of dashes along the ground. These were executed first with the rotor removed, then at just short of flying speed, and finally in a series of short hops to get the feel of things. The combination of their first flight and their first solo followed almost immediately.

The machine's military career was meteoric, to put it mildly, before the whole fleet, like the Ten Green Bottles, was consigned to a dustbin.

Perhaps its zenith was when one adventurous pilot, affectionately known as Mangle-toes, with possibly more daring than sense, tried to see how high he could get. He had achieved the dizzy altitude of 10,000 feet when, balanced precariously on his saddle, clutching at the handlebars and not daring to look down, he had an uncomfortably close encounter with a passing airliner. The resulting radio call to London ATC almost had its Captain grounded for life—'*London, can you advise? There's a goblin riding a bicycle outside my window and he's waving to me!*'

Shortly afterwards, the autogyrist, intoxicated by his own skill, was putting on a private flying display over Bulford Strip when he forgot that an autogyro, even more than a helicopter, needs an airflow through its disc. Executing a dazzling turn downwind, he found himself, much to his surprise, sitting on the damp grass in front of his admiring audience with the rotor lying across his lap. You, Oh my best beloved, will of course always remember that air speed and ground speed are not necessarily synonymous!

The other pilot, a somewhat skeletal figure aptly called Dem Bones, fared little better. His first humiliation came when, downwind in the circuit, his engine seized. Down he fluttered like a wounded crow and plumped into a field being ploughed by a local worthy. Never a master of the autorotative landing, he bounced a couple of times and then flipped over upside-down. Balanced on his head in the mud, his bottom ignominiously in the air and the machine strapped firmly to it, he struggled desperately to shrug off his appendage as it poured petrol over him via the near red-hot engine. The ploughman passed once and then again before Dem Bones shook off the wreckage and gave chase angrily. Finally he overtook the tractor and brought it to a reluctant halt. Standing in front of it, a picture of indignation, fingers extended palm upwards on outstretched arm towards the little heap of smoking tubing, he rounded on the driver and demanded furiously 'Why didn't you stop and help? I might have been burned alive!'

'Oh!' said the worthy, lighting his pipe amid shimmying petrol fumes 'Were youm in trouble? I thought as how youm were just practisin'!'

Sometime later, now fully qualified with about ten hours and one crash under his belt, Dem Bones was attached to my Flight for practical trials. Entering into the spirit of things, I immediately packed him off to Cornwall in a Landrover with his machine in the boot, to take part in a brigade amphibious assault exercise. He was to have been launched into the assault from the prow of some vessel, but the Navy took one look at him and his machine and demurred. In the end he had to make believe from a nearby headland instead. His task was to lead the assault and do the beach reconnaissance.

H hour duly arrived, and he took off in the grey dawn light to join the first wave of assault craft ploughing their way grimly towards the shore. Spearheading the assault, he whined in over the beach like an angry mosquito—but there his part in the affair terminated somewhat abruptly. You remember Mangle-toes'

The original 'Hear no evil, see no evil, speak no evil' aviators on No 1 Autogyro Course, December 1962: Messrs Manktelow, Warburton and Deane

undignified discovery that ground speed alone does not sustain flight? Well there is a very similar phenomenon called wind shear — and it is particularly prevalent near cliffs. Dem Bones momentarily hung unsupported in the air and then 'hit the beach' more literally than he had intended. His velocipede disintegrated around him, and he himself described a graceful arc through the air before plummeting headfirst into the sand.

Some people always land on their feet. Dem Bones, head buried in the sand, tail in the air yet again, did just that, if only metaphorically. His arrival, like the arrow in the Strongbow adverts, happened to terminate on the doorstep of the exercise medical tent and at the feet of the doctor in charge. Pulling the casualty out of the ground by the seat of his pants, the MO unhesitatingly diagnosed dehydration, prescribed stimulant and broached the medicinal brandy. Thereafter, he and his unexpected guest watched the rest of the assault, glass in hand in a haze of mutual alcoholic camaraderie, from the comfort of deck chairs.

So ended another step forward in Army aviation.

*There will be many more, oh my best beloved, and when they come your way, grasp the opportunity with both hands—but, while you are dicing with the latest phenomena, be it microlight or electronic wizardry, always remember the basic principle: what goes up, must come down.*

# FOOLS RUSH IN...

One of the joys of a military career, Oh My Best Beloved, is the ridiculous situations in which one frequently finds oneself. I joined my battalion from Sandhurst while it was in the final throes of hastily packing up before flying to Kenya to deal with the Mau Mau rebellion that had just broken out. We left three days later in a chartered fleet of Avro Yorks from Blackbushe Airport.

The situation in Kenya was tense, the papers and briefings had been full of gang raids, brutal murders and massacres. The fact that we were flying at all was some measure of the urgency of the situation as this was in the infancy of air trooping and the normal mode of travel was by troop ship. Our arrival at Eastleigh airport, Nairobi, was notable in that we leapt out of our aircraft, weapons at the ready—in roughly the same way as a stick of soldiers would from a helicopter in Northern Ireland today—much to the amazement of the laconic airport staff.

Once we realised that we were not about to be riddled with machine gun fire, we took over vehicles which were neatly lined up waiting for us. I was issued with a Landrover (stripped of roof and windscreen), two 3-tonners and a map. With 'Poacher' Saunders my batman driving and my new platoon behind me we set off for the battalion camp near Thompson's Falls some 200 miles away.

The tarmac ended at Muthaiga on the northern outskirts of Nairobi; thereafter it seemed to us that anything could happen on the dusty, corrugated murram road that wound through the African landscape. At every turn we expected hordes of chanting savages brandishing assagais and shields to fall murderously upon us; we were surprised and a little disappointed when nothing happened. Nevertheless, at our first break, the little convoy skidded to a grinding halt off the road in a cloud of red dust. To orders barked by the redoubtable Sergeant Kay, figures dashed off through the bushes to take up defensive positions.

I was most impressed. I had never seen anything quite like it before, even at Sandhurst—rrounded by swarms of pot-bellied little children who stood silently, fingers in dribbling mouths, staring at us in wide-eyed wonder and amazement. An old man passed us by wearing an ancient mackintosh tied round his waist with string, carrying a spear on his shoulder and driving an emaciated looking cow in front of him. He raised his battered homburg politely and said 'Jambo Bwana, habare yaco!' (Good day, sir, how are you?). Embarrassed, we cut short our stop and motored on.

With a mile or two to go, a pall of smoke appeared on the horizon ahead. The nearer we got, the stronger grew the suspicion that it came from our destination. The smoke quickly thickened into a towering column and the smell of fire was all about us in the air. I stopped my little column to study my map more closely and assess the situation. This time the sentries were dispatched in earnest and the rest of the platoon stood ready for instant action. Any lingering doubts were quickly dispelled when the crouching figures of a man and a woman ran out of a bush towards us waving frantically. I hoped that Sergeant Kay would restrain his enthusiasm and not open fire as they were clearly white.

On closer inspection, the pair turned out to be my epitome of Kenya settlers. He was tall and had a florid weather-beaten face framed by a white, neatly clipped, George V moustache and beard. He wore a khaki safari suit and a bush hat with a leopard skin hatband and carried a sporting Mauser rifle. She was slim, maturely good looking and also wore khaki, which somehow complimented her sun-browned face and sparkling blue eyes. It later transpired that he was a retired admiral and she his most recent mistress, lending truth to the then current saying 'Are you married or do you live in Kenya?'.

'Don't go on', he warned, 'You'll walk straight into hell. The camp is under attack. It's ablaze and there's shot and shell going off all over the place, I doubt there's anyone left alive by now.'

I knew that only our small advance party was in residence at the camp. Mine was the lead party of the battalion, so it was all up to me.

I squared my shoulders. This was it! I was faced with the reliefs of Mafeking, Khartoum and Rorke's Drift all rolled into one.

Sergeant Kay was way ahead of me. By the time the admiral had finished his story, sentries had been posted to guard the vehicles and civilians and the platoon had been deployed in classical arrowhead formation at the side of the road. We moved off through the bush to join battle.

As we pressed forward I could hear the crack of sporadic musketry. Smoke drifted round us and I suspected I could smell burning flesh. We broke out from the trees to an appalling sight. The whole camp was well ablaze. There was smoke and fire everywhere and we could see the silhouettes of figures against the flames, dashing hither and thither. Clearly either panic had set in among the defenders or the enemy was already in among them. We fixed bayonets and I drew my .38 pistol. Fanning out, we broke into a steady run, hoping we were not too late.

The first person I came across was Bill Kill, the Quartermaster. His face was blackened, he had a wild look in his eyes and he seemed on his last legs. He straightened up when he saw us and a look of amazement came over his face, which I mistook for relief.

'What the bloody hell are you lot playing at?' he demanded, eyeing our gleaming bayonets, 'Stop buggering about and lend a hand—and watch out by the ration tent, there's hot tins of bully beef and peas exploding all over the place'.

So passed my moment of glory. This was not a last-ditch stand by valiant defenders. There was not even an enemy! Some dolt had dropped a fag-end in the dry grass and set the place on fire. I surreptitiously holstered my pistol, shamefacedly hoping nobody had noticed it; the lads did the same with their bayonets and we got on with salvaging what we could from the flames.

The campaign that followed this rude opening was like something out of a storybook. I must be one of the few serving soldiers who, on jungle patrol, has had a spear thrown at him in anger and been chased at regular intervals by angry elephants, rhino and buffalo, not to mention an ostrich. It also planted the seed of my ambition to go flying. It all started with a Peepal tree.

The Company was based near the forest fringe on the southern slopes of Mt Kenya at the time. Our aviation needs were served by the Kenya Police Air Wing, flying Piper Cubs, but the nearest airstrip was at Nakuru, miles away. This fact was very nearly my downfall.

'Build me an airfield', said my revered Company Commander out of the blue one day.

I gulped. Anyone else might have been joking, but he had not got the nickname Captain Queeg (of Caine Mutiny fame) for nothing. Only a short while before, I had been invited to make him a football pitch in the middle of the bush—and I made the mistake of laughing heartily.

The area selected was the flat top of a low ridge emerging from the forest. I shared the site with the police, who were building a detention centre using Mau Mau terrorist prisoners as labour. Some 200 local villagers were mustered; under my inexpert direction they cleared the bush with pangas and levelled the ground with mattocks. Then, in clouds of dust and to the accompaniment of chanted litanies in glorious African harmony, they stomped up and down in their bare feet to pack down the surface. So much for bulldozers and steam rollers. The job was done.

The first landing was a cause for celebration. The whole labour force, swollen to near double in size and armed with jugs of *pombe* (a lethal millet beer), turned out for the occasion, jabbering excitedly. The pilot was one Punch Bearcroft, an intrepid one-armed aviator who I have mentioned in a previous tale. Unlike you, oh my best beloved, he had never heard of 'Density Altitude' so my miserable strip at some 10,000 feet held no fears for him. He came in to a perfect three point landing to the accompaniment of Oohs! and Aahs! like those you hear with the rockets on Guy Fawkes Night.

'How was it?' I asked proudly.

'All right, but I'll never get off again over that tree', he replied pointing at an enormous, gnarled specimen off the end of the strip, 'It'll have to go'.

The prospect of felling the giant even with power saws, let alone pangas, was appalling; then I remembered the boxes of gun-cotton stored in the company ammunition compound. I hurried back to the camp, selected a crate of gun-cotton, a reel of fuse, a box of primers and one of detonators and staggered back triumphantly with my load. The onlookers settled back comfortably with their jugs. clearly there was further entertainment on the programme.

My knowledge of explosives and demolitions was limited to a brief lecture during my platoon commander's course at the School of Infantry, through which I had probably slept anyway. I eyed my adversary wondering where to start. The huge bole forked about six feet above the ground and there was a gaping hole in the fork that disappeared down into the trunk—its Achilles Heel!

I levered the lid off the crate to reveal my first sight of real, live gun-cotton. Carefully prizing out a block, I inserted a primer, crimped a detonator onto the end of the fuse and then (was it 6 feet a second or 6 seconds a foot?) cut off what seemed a reasonable length. I carefully plugged the detonator into the primer and gently dropped the block into the hole. The whole lot, fuse and all, disappeared into the depth. Sweating, I made another charge and tried again, with the same result. By the time I had succeeded in placing a charge with the end of the fuse showing, the crate and the two boxes were half empty. It seemed rather pointless carrying the remainder back to camp (besides it really was a big tree), so I emptied the rest of the crate into the hole, threw in the rest of the primers and detonators for good measure and lit the fuse.

The one part of the lecture I could remember was 'Never run from the scene—you might fall. Walk!'

CLEARLY THERE WAS FURTHER ENTERTAINMENT ON THE PROGRAMME

I walked away. Behind me the burning fuse hissed loudly like a giant rocket racing towards I knew not what. As my brain struggled with vague calculations of fuse length and burning time, my walk got faster and faster until, I am ashamed to say, I broke into an Olympic sprint. Behind me, there was an enormous eruption. I looked back over my shoulder as I ran, to see what looked like a nuclear mushroom and huge chunks of gleaming white timber floating through the air in apparent slow motion. I thanked God for my cowardice.

The demolition was a brilliant success. When the dust settled, there was nothing but a hole in the ground with some brushwood round it. Also gone were the villagers, fled in terror into the forest, and with them several score Mau Mau prisoners and their guards never to be seen again.

Punch Bearcroft departed, well pleased, but I had some explaining to do.

*What is the connection with flight safety, oh my best beloved? None really. Only that fools rush in where angels fear to tread.*

# LOOK BEFORE YOU LEAP

What goes up must come down, but remember, oh my best beloved, that it is not always how you come down but where you do it that matters. Those of you who have mastered the skill of alighting like thistledown on anything from a pad to a pinnacle should be aware that, even with that skill, there are pitfalls for the unwary returning to terra firma.

You may not have heard of the Sioux pilot who landed in a dry wadi bed in the arid desert of Sharjah, only to have his aircraft washed away by a flash flood, or the Auster pilot who landed on a deserted beach for a swim, but was unable to restart the aircraft before it was overtaken by the tide. They, and many others like them, are still around.

I was tasked once on exercise with surveillance of a length of the Cornish coast, to watch out for submarine-launched raiding parties of Special Boat Service

saboteurs. After some hours of droning up and down looking out to sea, it dawned on me that the job could be done far more effectively and economically by sitting on the cliff top with a pair of binoculars (it is sometimes difficult to remember that a helicopter is a means to an end, not an end in itself).

Looking round for a suitable vantage point, my eyes lit on an old war-time pillbox, perched on the edge of the cliff above a delightful picture-postcard fishing village. Skillfully I parked my Skeeter on the roof. I was just settling back comfortably in my seat, when to my amazement a naked girl dashed out from underneath, closely followed by an equally nude youth; together they fled down the path to the village, bare cheeks bouncing in the sunlight.

The sight intrigued me, and that evening in the village pub I heard the full tale. Unbeknown to me, the local Casanova had selected the same pillbox for his latest amorous adventure. Passions rose high, but as their 'moment critique' arrived, so did I—on the roof just above them. It is hard to imagine the acoustic effect in an empty chamber of a Gipsy Major engine suddenly at full bore six foot above your head when you are least expecting it. Otherwise engaged as they were, it was devastating. The terrified girl burst into hysterics and, nakedness forgotten in the panic, bolted—closely pursued by her equally shaken inamorata. My part in the affair earned me and my crew free drinks for the rest of the night from a delighted clientele.

Sod's Law has little respect for rank or dignity, oh my best beloved, so it proved at the end of a major exercise when the local Aviation Commander mustered all his officers in the field to address them. The spot selected was below an embankment on a bend of a disused railway line, which formed a natural stage. For the maximum dramatic effect he arrived in a Skeeter, landed on the embankment astride the rusty line, and stepped out to address the assembled multitude below him.

He had barely got into his stride when slight vibrations underfoot and a distant whistle made him hesitate in mid-sentence before pressing gamely on. The vibration increased and with it came the unmistakable sound of a train. His audience lost their attentive expressions and began to look round and whisper among themselves, while his own flow of words gradually trailed to a halt. He stood there mouth open, gaping disbelievingly for a long moment; suddenly galvanised into action as the truth sank in, he flung himself back into the driving seat to try to get clear of the track.

The Skeeter was never renowned for easy starting, especially in an emergency. A cylinder full of misfired starter-cartridges later, the aircraft was engulfed in a cloud of acrid cordite smoke, but the engine had not even coughed. By then a leviathan had hove into sight only half a mile away, roaring into the bend at speed. Abandoning his sinking ship, the Captain leapt overboard and slid down the embankment to safety among his officers. Orders, suggestions and counter suggestions were flowing freely, but being all chiefs and no Indians, nobody actually did anything. As the moment of inevitable disaster arrived all eyes were fixed on the Skeeter. A stillness of almost sensual anticipation engulfed them. They held their breath—and the Hamburg express thundered by on an unnoticed, parallel track.

Cavalry officers have always been noted for *sangfroid* and quick thinking. One such officer showed these qualities to an exceptional degree when taking a high-ranking passenger to an important function. The trip was planned to near perfection; the pick-up of the resplendent passenger went well, and they arrived overhead his destination on the dot of time. Looking down at the scene below, they could see magnificent uniforms mingling with gay coloured dresses and Ascot hats on the lawn of the imposing headquarters. A band was drawn up on one side of a red carpet that led the short distance to an H neatly laid out on the manicured grass.

All appeared to be in readiness to receive the great man and a sea of white faces looked up at them in welcome as they arrived overhead—but there was one snag. Clearly if the helicopter landed on the H, the carpet would roll up like a spring in the down-wash; all the hats, and probably most of the dresses, would blow away and the big drummer would spin off uncontrollably through the ranks carving a swathe like a runaway battering ram. The pilot explained the problem to his passenger and quickly looked round for an alternative landing place.

The only possibility that presented itself was a tennis court a little distance away. Though a tight squeeze, it was feasible, but he dare not close down for fear of the drooping blades striking the tennis-net posts. As he descended, he briefed his passenger: the General would have to get out when they landed and kneel by the aircraft, while the helicopter took off again to clear the court for the reception.

All went comparatively well on landing and lift off, though the General —engulfed in a swirling storm of red clay dust—clearly had some difficulty maintaining his dignity while on his knees. He clutched his hat with one hand and manipulated the gleaming silver sabre dangling from his scarlet sash with the other.

Looking down, the pilot saw the reception party scurrying unceremoniously to the new RV. He watched the General get to his feet, cram his hat back onto his ruffled head, dust down his blues with thrashing hands and then stride towards the gate in the surrounding, high, chain-link fence.

There the tableau froze—with the General on one side of the wire and the reception party on the other. It was then that the awful truth dawned on the pilot and he realised the significance of there being no tennis-net strung across the

court. Tennis was not in season, the court was locked and nobody had the key!

*Perhaps by now you will have got my message, oh my best beloved: namely that time spent in reconnaissance is seldom wasted.*

# PUT THE OX TO THE PLOUGH

You may remember the moral of the last tale, oh my best beloved, that the helicopter was a means to an end rather than an end in itself. Many and varied are the 'ends' that the helicopter can be a 'means to', provided you use your imagination and, although not many pilots can be described as intellectuals, few can be accused of lacking imagination.

Some uses of the helicopter, though perfectly legitimate and reasonable, require a little tact and diplomacy in their execution, as was painfully discovered by a young officer some years ago.

In a moment of rare generosity his grandmother offered him her splendid, antique grandfather clock, which he had long coveted. Determined to strike while the iron was hot (and before he committed another of his frequent faux pas which would inevitably result in the offer being withdrawn) he cast around for the quickest way of collecting the treasure before she changed her mind. Clearly it would never fit into his sporty little car, but fortunately Her Majesty conveniently provided a wide range of vehicular transport for the job, and he carefully weighed up the pros and cons of each.

It would fit with difficulty into a Landrover, but the antique case and delicate mechanism would surely get damaged bouncing along the country roads. The same would apply to a 4 ton truck, and besides, that would be decided overkill.

It dawned on him that, with the back seat in the stretcher position, the old clock would fit snugly across the back of a Scout with its top and tail nestling in the door bulges.

The next day he had to take a passenger to the East coast; a very small diversion on the empty return trip would take him over his grandmother's house. It was a heaven-sent opportunity and without further ado he made the diversion.

Not surprisingly, the unexpected landing of a helicopter in a small field opposite the house on the edge of town attracted some attention. Even more interesting was the sight of a figure emerging from the helicopter, crossing the road and entering the house but the sight of the same figure re-emerging, staggering under a large antique grandfather clock was too much for one (not so innocent) bystander. He raised a Pentax camera to his eye, attracted the officer's attention with a hail and snapped the scene for posterity, before offering to lend a hand. Between them they loaded the clock into the Scout, secured it firmly in place and then, after a few jocular questions and equally light-hearted replies, the pilot thanked the Good Samaritan for his help and continued on his way.

Now there is nothing wrong with what he had done, just the way he went about it; in particular, with his unwitting choice of friends. Banner headlines appeared on the front page of the Daily Mirror the following morning, accompanied by a clear and unmistakable photograph of himself, with his timepiece on his shoulder and the helicopter in the background. This, together with a choice selection of out-of-context quotes, gave him cause for misgiving and the uncharitable reaction of his masters confirmed his worst fears.

Indiscretions have a habit of compounding themselves, so beware. Many years ago I was detached from the UK to Hameln for a four-month trial of a Sapper Air Troop. My newly-wed wife, bored with the solitary life at home, came and stayed with my cousin, the Engineering Officer in Hildesheim. Conveniently, I had to take my Skeeter there for servicing over a weekend. During dinner he asked if I had ever flown my wife. On learning that I had not, the 'serpent' suggested that I should take her with me on the return trip to Hameln. Foolishly I agreed, and between us we hatched a plot for the following morning. He would take her to the edge of town, where I would pick her up and fly her to Hameln, dropping her off on the outskirts before landing in barracks. Simple and foolproof.

To begin with all went well and, despite the bad weather, her first and only flight was clearly enthralling. The plain stretched out below like a patchwork carpet; a toy train, puffing white smoke, threaded its way lacing the squares together. Red roofs and white mine diggings were sprinkled in a bright pattern across the scene. Perched on a pinnacle, Schloss Marienburg appeared towering out of the gathering ground mist—a fairy tale castle, its turrets scraping the bottom of the lowering cloud base. While my wife was clearly thrilled and bubbling over with the experience, I was nervously peering ahead into the gathering gloom. The Wesergebirge hills, the low cloud, the fluffy ground mist and the steady drizzle undoubtedly blended together somewhere ahead into a thoroughly unpleasant cocktail.

This was no time to be caught floundering around in the murk. I had to unload my wife. I could not take her back, so I decided to drop her off by the main road and let her hitch the rest of the way, while I continued on alone. There was not much traffic on the road so, ever gallant, I decided to find a suitable car, flag it down and get her a lift. I found a comfortable-looking black limousine, flew alongside and began signalling the driver. My concentration and awareness was clearly not all that they should have been, because it was some moments before I realised that he was dressed in khaki. A hasty glance at the number plate confirmed my worst fears—beside it a telltale red plate sprinkled liberally with silver stars bore witness to the seniority of a figure in the back, hidden behind an open newspaper. Badly shaken, I peeled hastily away and completed the sortie uneventfully by air.

You may never have had the privilege of attending a rural Arab sheik's council, oh my best beloved. Imagine the scorching, eye-searing heat of the Arabian sun beating down on dusty, rocky hills. You escape the sun through an entrance in the massively thick mud walls of a 'Beau Geste' fort into a dark labyrinth of rooms, stairways and courtyards. All around lounge silent, wild, savage-looking men, colourfully robed and turbaned, their chests criss-crossed with full bandoliers, curved kunjas in their belts and an assortment of weapons in their hands. They are the sheik's bodyguard and they eye you scornfully, making you feel decidedly small and vulnerable.

You are escorted into the comparatively cool shade of a large upper room. All round are high, unglazed windows which catch a cooling breeze. At the far end, sitting cross-legged on the floor is the sheik himself, flanked by his close advisors. He looks disinterested in the proceedings and sucks occasionally at the mouthpiece of the hubble-bubble pipe standing in front of him, its bowl tended by a young lad. Visitors and plaintiffs sit around the walls, leaving the centre of the floor clear. Most have one cheek bulging grotesquely with a plug of *quat* (a chewing-leaf drug) and you wonder how stable they are. You find a space among them and sit down.

A 'Beau Geste' fort

The room is in complete silence, yet is somehow charged with excitement. A small terracotta bowl is brought in. It contains live coals with a sprinkling of sandalwood chips and herbs; a heady curl of aromatic smoke spirals up from it. The bowl is passed from hand to hand around the circle. Each in turn places it on the floor between his crossed legs, pulls his *sheemagh* (shawl), tent-like over his head, shoulders and knees, and steeps himself in the fragrance for a moment or two before emerging and passing on the bowl.

Charged with anticipation, the silence continues. Nothing happens for a long time until, apparently unbidden, someone gets up, walks down the room and squats in front of the sheik.

Wild-looking men firing their rifles, hopefully in welcome

After a suitable pause the sheik is passed a scrap of paper. He takes it and, without even glancing at it, hands it to his wazir, who occasionally murmurs something in his ear. Nothing is said, perhaps there

Bin Said inspecting a guard of honour
of the local militia

is a nod and then the plaintiff returns to his place; his petition has been accepted. After a long pause, another man steps forward. The procedure goes on interminably and is still going on when you leave, wondering if your spokesman has achieved, or even done, anything.

I once had the interesting experience of providing the actual council chamber for such meetings—a Scout helicopter!

In 1967 Colonel Grey, the British commandant of the Hadramout Bedouin Legion was murdered out of revenge by two renegade soldiers, who had been thrown out of the regiment for theft. Bin Said, the state secretary of Wahadi, was determined that they should be brought to justice and the 5th Battalion the Federal Regular Army, supported by 8 Flight AAC, were detached to help him catch the culprits. For the next week there followed a daily routine of visits into the hinterland to seek the help of the local sheiks and villagers. We set out each morning in three helicopters. The first, flown by me, carried Bin Said, Quaid (Lt Col) Ali Abdullah (the CO of 5 FRA) and Major Tim Goschen, a young Hussar officer, who was Bin Said's British political advisor.

The second (armed with two fixed forward-firing GPMGs) was flown by my 2IC, Captain Robin Grist,

Setting up the council. Maj Tom Goschen assists

Bin Said enthroned with his chokra in attendance. Sgt Bailey and the author look on

and carried an Air Trooper and two armed Arab soldiers. Sergeant Bill Bailey brought up the rear carrying two more soldiers, Bin Said's *chokra* (servant boy) and his hubble-bubble pipe.

At some of the places we visited there was a house (appropriate to Bin Said's rank) in which he could hold his council, but in many cases there was not, so we set up in the open. The Scouts were landed a little apart, preferably on high ground, with the GPMGs pointing roughly in the right direction to cover us. The rotors were kept turning until Bin Said gave the word that the reception was friendly. This was difficult to determine as, on landing, crowds of wild looking armed men would pour up the hill towards us, keening loudly and firing their rifles into the air in welcome. Until dissuaded from doing so, Bin Said had an upsetting habit of replying with an uncontrolled burst of Kalashnikov fire through the rotor blades.

Bin Said sat on the floor in the back of the Scout looking out over the side, his pipe burning beside him, his chokra behind him, reaching out and turning the coals. Quaid Ali, acting as his deputed wazir, sat on the ground to one side of him, Tim Goschen sat on the other and the crowd squatted in a hollow square around them. I stood behind the helicopter, ready to jump in if things turned nasty; the others stood by their Scouts trying to look as formidable as such a small group could. Business was conducted in silence as usual. I have yet to discover when, or how, our message was put across, but the Scout was a resounding success as a council chamber.

The two murderers were later caught and beheaded.

Shortly after this, SSgt Johnny Baulcomb AAC of 10 Flight and his passenger, Maj Peter Gooch of the Light Infantry, were murdered on landing in a Scout at Meifa on a roughly similar mission, and their aircraft was put to the torch.

Bin Said and Maj Tim Goschen were subsequently both killed by a bomb placed in an Aden Airways Dakota.

After the British left Aden in 1967, Quaid Ali was branded a traitor by the new Communist government and had to flee the country. He was killed two years later on a raid back across his border.

I once had a delightfully vague friend in the Royal Naval flight safety industry. His reply when I asked him if he still flew, gave me food for thought. 'Good God, no', he said, 'The third time my Chief Petty Officer had to tell me that I had left my car lights on in the car park, I gave up flying for good'.

Many years before that, I knew an equally delightful and vague Gunner pilot in 651 Squadron, when it was stationed at Middle Wallop. He lived in a charming cottage in Shrewton, where his wife was a leading light in the donkey-walloping society. They had one car between them and when she needed it (which was frequently) he got a lift into work with a friend.

He was settling behind his desk one morning when, on reaching into his pocket for a packet of cigarettes, his fingers touched the car keys.

'Oh my God!' he cried, leaping to his feet. 'Sally's meant to be going to an important meeting today and I've brought the wretched car keys to work with me!'

Vague he might have been but he was a man of action in a crisis. He shot out of his office, leapt into an Auster VI (yes, my best beloved, it was long before your time), started up, taxied out, took off and flew to Shrewton as fast as he could. When he got there, he buzzed the house until his wife came out into the garden. He then dived down and threw the keys out of the window with a note attached which read: 'Sorry about the keys, I hope you're not late for your Pony Club meeting'.

He watched her pick up the keys and wave and then returned to Wallop and his office, well pleased with his resourcefulness. He had hardly sat down at his desk again when the telephone rang. It was his wife, and she said:

'Darling, whatever are you up to? The meeting is tomorrow and besides, you've got the car!'

Just at that moment the Squadron Sergeant Major popped his head round the door with a grin and said: 'Excuse me, sir, but you've left your headlights on again. I couldn't turn them off for you this time, 'cos the car's locked.'

*Remember, oh my best beloved, that the aeroplane is a means to an end, not an end in itself, but give a little thought as to how and when you use it.*

# DEJA VU

You may know the story of the old Jewish businessman who took his five-year-old son to his office to start his business education. Once there, he hoisted the little fellow up onto a tall filing cabinet and playfully said 'Jomp Villie, I'll ketch you'. Trustingly, the little lad flung himself gleefully off the pinnacle towards his father's open arms. As he did so, the old man stepped smartly back and the little mite crashed painfully onto the stone floor and lay there sobbing pitifully. His father bent down, tapped him on the shoulder and said 'Dare you are, ma boy. Your furst lesson in beesiness—*never trost anybody!*'

Those of you, oh my best beloved, who are just starting in the flying business would do well to heed that lesson and keep a wary eye on your instructor!

It happened half way through my pilot course on Austers. My new instructor was a revered, ex-infantry Glider Pilot; he had glided into Arnhem and several other traumatic places, and was on about his third bound volume of logbooks. We had just completed what, for him, must have been a rather dull period of upper air work. We were still at about 4,000 feet, when he turned to me and said 'You've done 'Fire in the air' haven't you?'

It meant nothing to me, and I shook my head.

'Oh', he said 'It's the quickest way down.'

He explained that, if you had a fire, you headed for the ground as fast as possible—switching off the fuel and electrics on the way — so as not to feed the flames, and side-slipping violently to blow them away from the cockpit. His whole attitude brightened and he demonstrated.

'FIRE IN THE AIR!' he shouted, mentally reverting to his infantry weapon-training days and the first 'Immediate Action' on the Bren Gun, 'SWITCHES OFF, FUEL OFF, THROTTLE CLOSED. MAYDAY, MAYDAY, MAYDAY. FULL LEFT PEDAL. PICK A FIELD...'

His hands darted round the cockpit going through the motions in an exaggerated pantomime as he went through his patter.

Deafened, frightened and sliding perilously off my wildly tilting seat, I hung desperately onto my door handle with both hands to stop myself falling across his lap as we fell like a brick, sideways towards the ground. As a hedge and a ploughed field came rushing up to meet us, his staccato patter ended with 'KICK HER STRAIGHT AND LEVEL, AND LAND.'

He pushed open the throttle to overshoot but, now that his voice had stopped, there was only an eerie silence except for the whistling of the wind in the rigging and the whirr of the windmilling propeller. We flopped into the plough, bounced and stopped dead.

I gazed in undisguised admiration at the man beside me. What a man! What a pilot! What a demonstration! And into a ploughed field too!

He ruined my illusion with an expletive. 'What the **** happened to the ****ing engine?'

'You turned off the fuel and the switches.' I volunteered innocently.

'Don't be a ...' His voice trailed away as his eyes disbelievingly followed my pointing finger.

'What do you know about carburettor icing?' he ventured pensively as we trudged, leaden-booted, across the wet plough towards the Pheasant Inn.

My blank expression gave its own answer. When we got there (the patron kindly opened the bar—it being something of an emergency), he explained over a soothing glass. By now, oh my best beloved, you may have noticed that real instructors never have any money or cigarettes in their pockets!

The Chief Flying Instructor, then a somewhat pedantic and humourless Wing Commander, arrived on the scene several pints and a packet of Players later.

'Well, what happened?' he said resignedly.

'Carburettor icing!' we announced in unison, standing precariously to attention, but I still had no idea what it meant.

You may not be familiar with the strange phenomenon of *déjà vu*, oh my best beloved?

Many years after this incident I found myself back at Wallop as OC Advanced Rotary Wing Flight. I was a Scout man myself, and could almost make a Scout talk, but ARW was equipped with Sioux.

When I took up the post, the only experience I had on Sioux was as a Scout instructor several years before, going to Gallorati in Italy to collect the first batch of Agusta Bells. I had never flown one before. My 'Spaghetti Bomber' conversion consisted of half an hour in the Agusta hangar with a non-English-speaking, Italian test pilot, being shown how to start and stop the Sioux, before setting out for England.

With the rusty memories of that trip as my expertise, one of my first tasks in ARW Flight was to do a student's Intermediate Handling Check. My victim got hopelessly lost low-level, droned around aimlessly and I got bored.

'Have you done low-level-engine-offs?' I asked. He shook his head.

'PRACTICE ENGINE FAILURE!' I said, entering into it with gusto. 'SWITCHES OFF. FUEL OFF. THROTTLE CLOSED. MAYDAY MAYDAY MAYDAY. PICK A FIELD STRAIGHT AHEAD. FLARE!'

I stopped talking and opened the throttle to overshoot...

There was a deathly silence but for the swishing of the wind and the whirring of the blades. We hurtled downwind and downslope like the Cresta Run, scattering sheep in all directions, before coming to rest just short of the hedge.

I caught a frankly admiring look in my student's eyes as I eased myself back in my seat. I wondered if he had a cigarette on him.

*That's 'déjà vu', oh my best beloved!*

# TO BEACHY HEAD BY WAY OF BANNOCKBURN

Navigation to precise limits can nowadays be a matter of a touch of a button, but it is worth remembering that even the best equipment can go wrong — and usually does, at inconvenient moments. My own navigation gear, the Mk 2 Eyeball (the Mk 1 is what the Good Lord provided, but mine has been modified by surgery), did just that only the other day.

I had an appointment for routine equipment servicing at Moorfields Eye Hospital in the City—the base workshops. I had been asked to leave my contact lenses out, so I went up to London by train wearing my spectacles. These are bifocal and as thick as the bottom of a beer bottle. Imagine walking round London wearing night vision goggles with the bottom segment out of focus and you have it.

Disaster struck at Waterloo station. In a hurry and unsighted, I completely missed the top step of the escalator, and stepped downwards into space travelling at some speed. Trying to catch up with myself, I broke into a fast sprint down the long drop in the general direction of the Bakerloo Line, like a Gurkha khud racer at full stretch. My first point of contact was the back of an enormous black gentleman immaculately dressed in a canary yellow suit and scarlet shirt.

Sixteen stone of ex-Barbarian rugby player in full flight takes some stopping. He failed, and we careered on together like an avalanche, gathering more and more unfortunate commuters on the way, a score or more of us ending in a fearful tangle of arms and legs on the floor at the bottom. When we sorted ourselves out, fortunately nobody seemed to have been hurt but my glasses were nowhere to be found. The rest of the journey, as embarrassing as it was difficult, was completed on the arm of a helpful old lady.

The same thing happening in the air can be equally embarrassing. Some time ago, when 651 Squadron was located at Debden (North of London), a very senior

General, his MA and his ADC turned up unexpectedly on the doorstep with pressing reasons to be got to Biggin Hill by the quickest possible means. The weather was appalling but a quick check showed Biggin to be in the clear.

There were only three pilots to hand, Mike and Ken (the Squadron Commander and his second in command, who between them had more hours than the Angel Gabriel) and Henry—a dashing young cavalryman, fresh out of the egg, who had only arrived from Wallop a couple of days before. There was no time for legal niceties; a snap decision was made—Mike would take the General, Ken the MA and young Henry would bring up the rear with the ADC. Three Auster VIs were wheeled out, and they climbed aboard. The little flight took off in the dank, dripping air, and winged its way south.

Following the railway line down a valley, the inevitable happened—the low cloud and the surrounding hills gradually merged. 'CLIMB, CLIMB, CLIMB' called Mike in desperation as he threw away his map, squeezed the final half horse power out of his Gipsy Major engine, pointed the nose up into the lumpy porridge above and pinned his faith in modern technology.

It was like missing the top step of the escalator and losing his glasses all rolled into one. Things quickly got out of hand and went from bad to worse. The sight of the general hanging from his straps beside him, his face pressed against the roof perspex, did little to encourage him. He was almost at his wit's end (desperately trying to dislodge the slip indicator ball, which was inextricably wedged at one end of its tube, while scanning his remaining three intoxicated flight instruments) when he broke cloud in one of the most unusual 'Unusual Attitudes' he had ever experienced. Not far away, another Auster tumbled out of the cloud in roughly the same manner. It was Ken. There was no sign of Henry and no sound from him on the radio. Nothing. Sadly they called up Biggin and informed them of the loss.

'Oh, he's here,' came the cheerful reply, 'He's just making the coffee. Do you want a word with him?'

It transpired that Henry, watching the other two disappearing into the cloud, had decided (discretion being the better part of valour) not to follow them. He may not have known much about instrument flying, but he did know London like the back of his hand. Down the Edgeware Road he went; down Park Lane and touched his cap at Her Majesty's front door, before turning left at Victoria and crossing the river at Vauxhall Bridge. Cutting the corner across the Oval, he joined the A20 and landed at Biggin Hill without a hair out of place—having given his passenger a very pleasant sightseeing tour of the metropolis.

*There must be a moral or two in this little tale, oh my best beloved. If nothing more, know your own limitations (and the other fellow's), and don't put all your eggs in one basket.*

# ALL FINGERS AND THUMBS

If you, or any of your friends, are contemplating a career in Army Aviation, oh my best beloved, read on. This salutary little tale may help you come to a decision.

Kin Maun Tint was small, petite and Burmese. He was said to be a prince of the royal blood, or anyway a prince of some sort. In this he was somewhat overshadowed during his time at the RMA Sandhurst as his intake also boasted a king. The square used to ring to the shrill, chilling tones of RSM JC Lord ('He's Lord up there, and I'm Lord down here!'). Every individual syllable, crisp and crystal clear, cut through the air like a rapier:

*'Mister King Hussein, sir—what are you doing with that rifle—cuddling it?'*

Poor Kin Maun Tint answered to plain, 'Mister Tint, sir'.

I first met up with Tint at equitation classes. He appeared, looking like a tiny china doll immaculately turned out from top to toe by Gieves. The eyes of the Corporal of Horse in charge lit on him with a mixture of stunned disbelief and mischievous joy. The preliminaries over, we were taken to saddle up our horses. There was a row of them—all roughly standard size except for one enormous grey called Pegasus, who towered above the rest. Inevitably, yet without apparent direction, Tint found himself paired off with the leviathan.

His attempts at saddling-up had us all surreptitiously watching out of the corner of our eyes. Our suppressed mirth was made even worse by the fact that the faintest sign of a grin, let alone a splutter, drew an instant, cutting rebuff from the straight-faced Corporal of Horse. Tint had clearly never been near a horse in his life before, let alone one about twice the size of the royal elephants — and they kneel down to be saddled and mounted.

After several abortive attempts at reaching up with the saddle, he realised the utter futility of this line of attack. He next tried throwing it, but only succeeded in giving himself a painful blow under the chin with one stirrup and Pegasus an equally painful crack in the eye with the other. At this point the Corporal of Horse relented somewhat. Wooden mounting steps were produced and the luckless Tint tried again.

By this time, Pegasus—a polite but knowing beast—had entered into the spirit of things. Every time Tint reached out towards him

LEANED AWAY WITHOUT APPARENTLY MOVING HIS FEET

from his precarious perch, saddle in hand, the horse leaned away just far enough to be out of reach. All other activity in the class ceased as instructor and students alike watched with admiration as Pegasus, without moving his feet, stretched Tint a little bit further on each attempt. Finally, and inevitably, Prince and saddle crashed face down in the urinated dust under the horse's belly. At last, with two students directed to push against Pegasus' offside, the job was done and a somewhat dishevelled Tint thankfully tightened and buckled up the girth and mounted. The rest of us followed suit and we moved off at the walk, line astern, Pegasus leading.

Those first few steps must have been sheer agony for poor Tint whose thighs were stretched apart in an exaggerated splits astride the horse's broad back. Fortunately (or perhaps not) that pain was as short-lived as the ride. Pegasus had assumed an uncharacteristic swaying gait, rather like a camel; Tint followed suit, clinging on to the pommel for dear life. After about five strides the horse let his breath out with an audible hiss, the girth went dead slack and the saddle—with Tint still attached—continued on round. For a brief moment Tint hung like a dewdrop under Pegasus' belly and then he crashed down onto his brand new bowler.

The dapper Kin Maun Tint's retirement from the equestrian field was a sad loss to the class. On the other hand, Pegasus, having learned that trick, went on to perfect it. His tour de force came when he tried it on the Assistant Adjutant, a diminutive Welsh Guardsman known as Badley-Bent. He deposited him—in full No 1 Dress Blues and sword—on his head, at the feet of the entire Academy as it formed up ready to march on for the Sovereign's parade dress rehearsal. Being

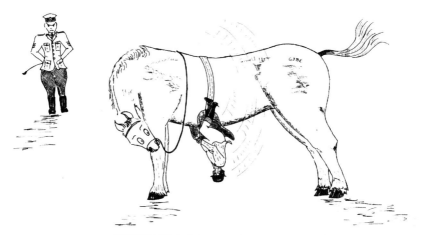

HANGING LIKE A DEWDROP UNDER THE LEVIATHAN

in the Colour Party, I was directly behind him and bore close witness to Pegasus' consummate skill.

In those days, one of the more enjoyable subjects at the RMA was D&M (Driving and Maintenance to the uninitiated, oh my best beloved). The driving side started on motorcycles and later progressed to that fine old military vehicle, the 15cwt Bedford truck of World War 2 desert fame.

The first day saw us on the MT square where, rather like at the equestrian class, a row of about twenty BSA 500 motorbikes were lined up at one end waiting for us. We 'numbered off' and fell in, smartly at attention, on the near side of our respective machine. By chance I was next to Kin Maun Tint. In front of us, beside a gleamingly polished machine, stood our instructor, SSgt Blair RE, impeccably dressed in despatch rider rig—jodhpurs, glistening motorcycle boots and a para-type helmet. He was a barrel of a man with a hoarse, Geordie accented voice which came across about as unintelligibly as a passing express train. He clearly assumed that 'all young gentlemen could already ride motorcycles' but this, as it happened, was not quite the case—anyway not as far as Tint was concerned.

'Right, Gin'lemen!' he roared in explanation, pointing at the various controls: 'The BSA 500. Hand brake. Clutch. Gear lever—one up, three down. Kick-start. Clear? Right, fifteen minutes round the square clockwise, practising changing gears. Start up and move off, No1 leading!' We all leapt smartly onto our kick-starters and the air was filled with smoke and the deafening roar of nineteen furiously revving 500cc. Nineteen? Yes, the twentieth was Kin Maun Tint's. He sat there dabbing pathetically at the starter with a dainty polished toecap.

'Put some weight on it, Mista Tint, sir!' bellowed Blair coming up behind him, 'Like this!' And he rammed his size 12, hobnailed boot down on the starter with the force of a battering ram. The effect was electric. The bike was in gear and it shot off with a roar, Tint clinging desperately to the handgrips and the rest of him flapping out behind like a pennant in the wind. The tighter he gripped, the wider he opened the throttle and away he went like John Gilpin at full gallop. Once again he reduced the whole class to stunned spectators.

The MT square at Sandhurst was about 150 yards long by 50 yards wide. One side was bounded by the gymnasium, the other by a birch wood and there was a collection of huts at each end. The bike accelerated down the wood straight with Tint gradually slipping down the off side until he lay along it like a Red Indian, one leg hitched over the saddle. The weight distribution was enough to drag the machine round in a U-bend at the far end and back onto the gymnasium straight, where Tint managed to clamber part way back into the saddle. The sight of us and a row of motorcycles looming up ahead was too much for him and he slipped back down again.

The bike executed another forced right turn but this time not a full U. It tore across our front, bounced across the grass and disappeared into the wood. Several crumpling thuds echoed from deeper and deeper among the trees. After the last one, the already tortured engine wound up to a steady and constant high-pitched scream. We found Tint, battered and torn, suspended in the foliage with his bike still roaring underneath him. Most of a box of Elastoplast and a good dusting down soon restored him to duty.

Tint had one more outing before motorcycling was added to his list of excused activities. This too came to an equally abrupt and dramatic end. I was just behind him on the road separating Old from New College when, for the first time, he managed to escape first gear. What gear he actually hit, I do not know but the bike leapt forward like a startled stag, leaving Tint stretched out on the pillion. Ahead of him two ancients from the band were trundling a handcart piled high with band instruments down the road.

The Royal Military Academy Band Corps, now sadly defunct, was the smallest corps in the British Army and its members were long past the age for heroics. On seeing Tint roaring towards them, these two worthies broke and ran leaving the cart to its own fate. Tint hit it amidships and at speed. For one brief, but unforgettable moment the whole ensemble, Tint, bike, cart and all the band instruments were airborn simultaneously before hitting the tarmac in a fearful cacophony of jangling sound. Once again the Elastoplast packet restored Tint to near normal but the band was reduced to fife and drum for some time afterwards.

Much of the movement to and from the various exercises at Sandhurst used to be executed in formation by bicycle. The Army bicycle of the day was made of heavy gauge steel piping and weighed half a ton. It had no gears, had a back-pedal braking system and was painted khaki. Company-strength crocodiles of cadets, furiously pedalling these velocipedes down the A30, entertained motorists and locals alike as they tried to back wheel the one behind or get a swagger stick through the spokes of the one ahead.

Being the RMA, everything had to be done in military fashion. There was a drill for everything and not least was Bicycle Drill. On our first attempt at it, the whole Company, under Company Sergeant Major Cyril Goman, paraded at the back of the square with their machines to perform this strange ritual.

On the command, 'RIGHT MARKERS', the chosen few, both hands on the grips, sprang to attention and marched out the regulation fifteen paces before crashing to a halt. 'GITORN PERIDE' brought the rest of us out in similar fashion to form one long single rank across the square. 'RIGHT DRESS', as well as the usual high speed foot shuffling, involved bouncing the heavy bicycle smartly into position using one hand on the bar.

The next order 'IN TWOS, NUMBAH' produced a melodious chorus of '1, 2, 1, 2, 1, 2' rippling down the rank. This was closely followed by 'WHEEL, HALF RIGHT, TURN' and then, 'IN TWOS, BY THE FRONT, WALK MARCH'. On this last somewhat obscure command, the whole line moved smartly off together, forming a crocodile in the process. Kin Maun Tint accomplished all these manoeuvres successfully but then came the difficult part! The next order, 'PREPARE TO MOUNT' involved watching the revolving pedals and picking the brief moment when the nearside one was in front, to leap on. Unfortunately this seldom coincided with the command, 'MOUNT'. Later, with practice, one learned to leap aboard, cowboy fashion, without touching the pedals at all, but on that first parade the need was not apparent. This time, Cyril, in knowing anticipation, screamed the word, 'MOUNT' with such ferocity that, tuned as we were to the word of command, we all unhesitatingly jumped together—and there the rot began. Those who landed with the pedal to the fore shot forward. Those bikes with it at the rear stopped dead, flinging the rider over the handlebars, face down onto the gravel with the man behind riding over him. The whole unwieldy column piled up on itself in an unimaginable tangle of tortured limbs and twisted metal under Cyril's admiring gaze.

By some happy or luckless chance, Kin Maun Tint's pedal had been at the front and he debouched at some speed out of the side of the melée. Now one would have thought that, whatever else an Asiatic could or could not do, they can all ride bicycles. Tint, quite clearly, could not. He wobbled, out of control, across the square at right angles to the intended direction of movement and, with a despairing scream, disappeared down the ornate flight of steps leading onto the sports field below. The sickening crunch of his arrival at the bottom was fortunately drowned by the groans of the wounded on the square.

*You may wonder what all this has to do with flying, oh my best beloved? It is simply that, if you don't have the aptitude, or you are accident prone, it might be to your advantage to turn your hand to other things.*

*On the other hand, the last I heard of Tint it appeared he was an Air Marshal in the Burmese Air Force.*